HOW TO BUILD AN IGLOO

AND OTHER SNOW SHELTERS

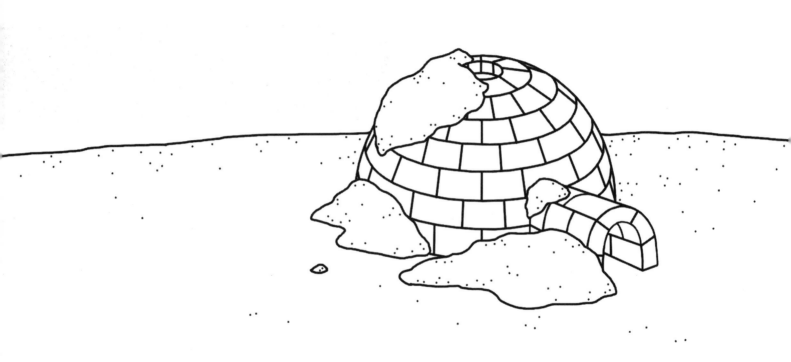

HOW TO BUILD AN IGLOO
AND OTHER SNOW SHELTERS

Norbert E. Yankielun

Illustrations by Amelia Bauer

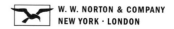
W. W. NORTON & COMPANY
NEW YORK · LONDON

Graphic concept by Andrew Tarcin

Copyright © 2007 by Norbert E. Yankielun
Illustrations copyright © 2007 by W. W. Norton &
Company, Inc.

For information about permission to reproduce
selections from this book, write to Permissions,
W. W. Norton & Company, Inc., 500 Fifth Avenue,
New York, NY 10110

Book design by Rubina Yeh
Composition by Ken Gross
Manufacturing by Courier Westford
Production Manager: Leeann Graham

Library of Congress Cataloging-in-Publication Data

Yankielun, Norbert E.
  How to build an igloo—and other snow shelters /
Norbert E. Yankielun ; illustrations by Amelia Bauer.
—1st ed.
          p.   cm.
  Includes bibliographical references and index.
  ISBN-13: 978-0-393-73215-3 (pbk.)
  ISBN-10: 0-393-73215-0 (pbk.)
  1. Igloos. 2. Mountain shelters. 3. Building, Ice
and snow. 4. Wilderness survival. 5. Snow—Thermal
properties. I. Title.

TH4890.Y36 2007
693'.91—dc22   2006101144

ISBN 13: 978-0-393-73215-3 (pbk.)
ISBN 10: 0-393-73215-0 (pbk.)

W. W. Norton & Company, Inc., 500 Fifth Avenue, New
York, N.Y. 10110
www.wwnorton.com
W. W. Norton & Company Ltd., Castle House, 75/76
Wells St., London W1T 3QT
    2 3 4 5 6 7 8 9 0

I dedicate this book to my parents, dear friends, and acquaintances who have given me love, inspiration, guidance, and moral support along the winding, snowy pathway that I have trod.

CONTENTS

INTRODUCTION

Nature is full of genius . . . so that not a snowflake escapes its fashioning hand. —HENRY DAVID THOREAU

There are lots of reasons to build a snow shelter. A snow shelter can be a serious survival refuge for people who work or play in the winter backcountry. It can be a fun social experience shared by friends, or a wonderful educational and inexpensive afternoon family project. This book provides guidance and plans for first-time backyard builders and experienced backcountry winter campers to successfully construct a wide variety of snow shelters.

Most of us think of snow in the simplest of terms: Delicate crystals of frozen water are formed high in the atmosphere, fall from the sky, and cover the ground with a blanket of white. Under closer examination, snow is an amazing and complex material. How does snow "happen"? How can a sturdy, weatherproof shelter be built from these light and delicate flakes that fall from the sky? How can something as cold as snow help keep a person relatively warm? How can snow be used to build practical shelter for backcountry survival or backyard recreation? To answer these questions, a basic understanding of snow science is a helpful first step.

THE SCIENCE OF SNOW

The field of snow science explores the complex interaction of atmospheric humidity, air and ground temperature, altitude, air pressure, wind velocity and direction, and even the degree of sunlight present. A detailed scientific

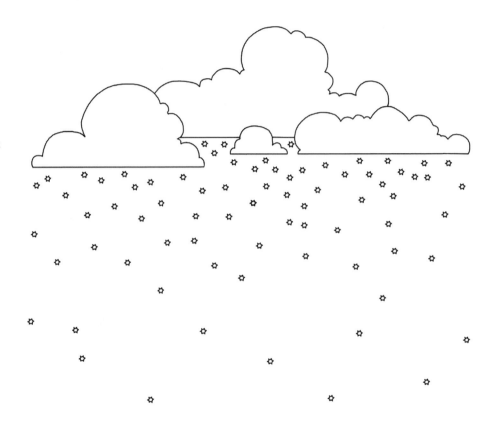

explanation would fill several textbooks. For an in-depth understanding it would require more than a passing knowledge of meteorology, chemistry, physics, and thermodynamics. Fortunately, only a simple understanding is helpful for snow shelter builders.

NATURAL SNOW

Snow forms from moisture in the atmosphere. The moisture in atmospheric clouds consists of a concentration of minute water droplets. These droplets formed by the condensation of water vapor onto minute particles—called *condensation nuclei*—including soil and dust that have been carried aloft. When the air temperature is below 32 degrees Fahrenheit (0 degrees Celsius), instead of forming water droplets around the nuclei, ice crystals form. If the temperature is extremely cold, ice crystals may form without the presence of nuclei. Once the initial crystal forms, the growth of a snowflake is dependent on the addition of water vapor molecules, obtained from liquid water droplets in the cloud or by means of minute water droplets freezing to the initial ice crystal as it falls through the atmosphere. If the air is cold enough throughout the time the crystal falls, a frozen snowflake will arrive at the ground. If the air is above freezing, the ice crystals may melt and become rain. Depending on the atmospheric conditions under which these snow crystals have formed, they can take on many different shapes, from elongated needles of ice, to six-sided platelets, to the familiar pointy star shape, and even frozen pellet-shaped blobs of ice. The shape of ice crystals in a snowstorm will determine the initial characteristics of a snowpack.

The different shapes and sizes of snow that form in the atmosphere. Left to right: elongated ice needle, eight-sided platelet, star, and frozen pellet-shaped blob.

MACHINE-MADE SNOW

Most ski mountain resorts produce machine-made, or artificial, snow to supplement natural snowfall. It is an excellent material for building recreational snow shelters. The two key ingredients needed to produce machine-made snow are water and cold temperatures. In one common snowmaking process, compressed air is mixed with water and forced through a nozzle of a snow gun at a high velocity to create tiny droplets. Under ideal conditions of temperature and humidity, these droplets travel through the air and freeze before hitting the ground. Usually, microscopic particles in the water stream act as *nucleators*, facilitating the snow-forming process. (A nucleator allows water vapor molecules a place to collect and freeze into an ice crystal that eventually becomes a snowflake. In the case of natural snow, bits of dust in the atmosphere act as nucleators.) Frequently, additional particles or non-toxic chemical nucleators are added to the water stream to further encourage the crystallization process.

The nature of the snow produced is greatly affected by air temperature, humidity, and the size of the droplets produced. Under ideal snowmaking conditions, the proportion of water to air introduced to the snow gun nozzle can vary the makeup of the artificial snow produced. Increasing the amount of water for a given amount of air typically produces a wetter, denser, and "sticky" snow. This type of snow makes a good base layer on a ski slope. By reducing the amount of water relative to a given amount of air, a lighter, less dense, dryer snow can be produced. This more powdery snow makes a great skiing surface, but is not necessarily usable for shelter construction. Once on the ground, the nature of the snow changes over time by skier traffic, grooming machines, air temperature, and exposure to the warming rays of the sun, transforming a machine-made snowpack into usable material for shelter construction.

SNOW AS AN INSULATOR

An insulator is a material that slows down the transfer of heat energy from a warm mass to a colder mass. Heat can be transferred by three methods: convection, conduction, and radiation.

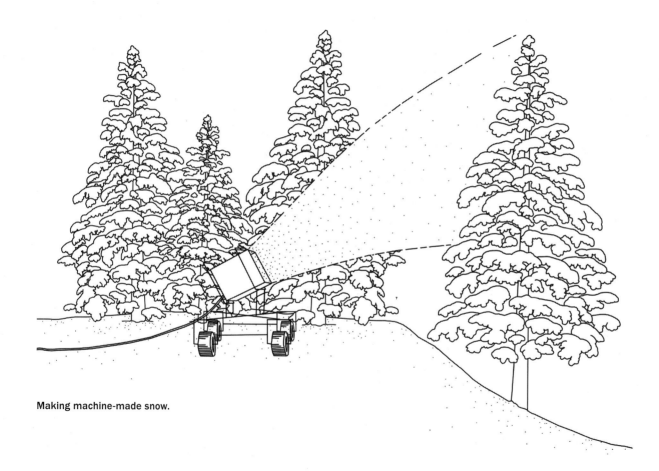

Making machine-made snow.

Convection transfers heat by the movement of air. Cool air warmed by a heat source rises, carrying away heat energy from the source. Blowing on a hot cup of cocoa cools it by convection. *Conduction* transfers heat away from a warm body by contact with a cold liquid or solid. Warm bare feet stepping on a cold floor are cooled by conduction. *Radiation* is the transfer of heat energy by electromagnetic waves and does not rely on solids, liquids, or gases for energy transfer. The sun provides heat energy to the earth across the vacuum of space from millions of miles away by means of radiation.

Snow best insulates against heat loss caused by convection. A fluffy layer of newly fallen snow has a large amount of air trapped between the snow crystals. This low-density snow may consist of about 10 percent ice and 90 percent air. The air trapped between the ice crystals gives snow its insulating property. This combination of snow crystals and trapped air acts in a similar way to goose down insulation in a ski jacket or sleeping bag. The air trapped in the tiny spaces between ice crystals does not permit easy conduction of body heat to the outside environment. It is estimated that 10 inches (25 centimeters) of freshly fallen snow has the same insulation value as 6 inches (15 centimeters) of fiberglass! A layer of cold, dry snow on the roof can help keep a house a bit warmer. A layer of snowcover can insulate the ground from frigid temperatures and protect plant roots and hibernating animals from freezing, even when the outside temperature is well below zero.

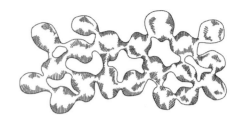

The volume of air trapped between ice grains creates the insulating property of snow.

When compacted by the wind or by hand, some of the air trapped between the snow crystals is squeezed out. This produces a more dense snow with a somewhat lower insulating value. Nevertheless, even densely compacted snow serves as a good insulator from convective heat loss.

Body heat generated by the occupants of a snow shelter warms the interior air through convection. The insulating property of snow inhibits the convective transfer of this heated air through the walls of the shelter to the outdoors. Trapped body heat can raise the air temperature inside a snow shelter several degrees above freezing, even when outside temperatures are well below zero.

METAMORPHOSIS

Snow crystals undergo nearly constant change in structure from the moment they form until they eventually completely melt or sublime. This process of change is called *metamorphosis*. Melting is the process by which water changes from a solid state (ice) into a liquid state (water). When ice sublimes it transforms directly from a solid state to a gaseous state (water vapor) without first becoming liquid water. An example of the process of sublimation can easily be seen in a home freezer. Notice how ice cubes appear to shrink in size after they have been refrigerated for several months. Since the freezer does not permit melting, the volume of the ice has shrunk because, over time, many of the water molecules have sublimated into water vapor, which is eventually dispersed into the atmosphere.

In nature, metamorphosis is driven by time; air; ground temperature; exposure to sunlight, wind, and humidity; additional precipitation; and even the weight and depth of additional snowfall. Metamorphosis affects the shape of the ice crystals as well as the density and how well the snowpack holds together.

Three basic mechanisms of snow metamorphosis exist: destructive, temperature gradient, and melt. In

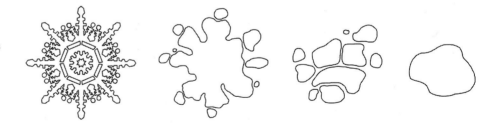

A sequence showing the metamorphosis of a single snowflake over time.

destructive metamorphosis, water vapor is released from the snowflakes. This release changes the sharp angular shape of snowflakes into rounded and irregularly shaped smooth ice grains. The released water vapor collects in the voids between nearby ice grains and begins to freeze. Ice bridges form and connect adjacent ice grains. The process whereby two ice grains become interconnected, or welded together, without the presence of liquid water, is called *sintering*. Sintering creates a dense, strong, cohesive snowpack. The process of sintering can be sped up by wind or mechanical compaction. Compressing a mitten-full of snow into a snowball is a form of manual compaction.

Temperature gradient metamorphosis occurs when there is a large temperature difference between the top and bottom of a snowpack. Since snow is a good insulator, the air temperature at the surface of the snowpack may be much colder than the temperature of the snow nearer the ground. This temperature difference, or gradient, encourages the downward movement of water vapor released from grains in the upper layer of the snowpack. This water vapor leads to the formation of *depth hoar*—large, loosely bonded crystals near the base of the snowpack. Depth hoar is sometimes called *sugar snow*.

The cycle of melting and freezing is responsible for *melt metamorphosis*. When the air temperature rises above freezing, melting snow releases liquid water, which is absorbed into the snowpack. When the air temperature again drops below freezing, the liquid water refreezes creating a denser snowpack of larger, irregular ice grains. After repeated melting and freezing cycles, the snowpack eventually becomes the loose "corn snow" typically encountered by spring skiers.

APPROPRIATE SNOW

Many types of shelters can be built from snow, including igloos, quinzees, slab shelters, and drift caves. Some can be built under a wide range of snow conditions. The major consideration is whether the consistency of the snow is structurally appropriate for the type of shelter desired. In some cases a bit of time and physical effort can change the snow into a usable consistency. Carefully consider this investment in time and effort, especially if in the backcountry or in a survival situation. For most types of snow shelters, a particular consistency of snow works best. It may be more efficient to modify your shelter design to meet snow conditions rather than attempt to modify snow conditions to create a particular type of shelter. The snow conditions that are best for construction of a variety of shelters are discussed in the following chapters.

DISCLAIMER

Because of the variability in the physical and structural characteristics of snow, shelter dimensions given in this book should be used only as general guidelines.

As with all outdoor activities, especially under winter conditions, inherent hazards exist. It is the personal responsibility of the reader to become knowledgeable about these risks and personally assume all responsibilities associated with them.

CHAPTER 1
PREPARATION BEFORE BUILDING

Be prepared. —BOY SCOUT MOTTO

Several items must be considered before venturing out into the cold and snowy winter and building a snow shelter. It is important to take care of the physical health of all participants, be aware of potential hazards, and have the right tools to do the job.

MAKING FRIENDS WITH WINTER

The same environmental ingredients that are essential to creating the snow that we use to build our structures—sub-freezing temperatures and water—can also cause a degree of discomfort and potentially lead to injury. Making "friends" with winter will assure that the snow shelter building experience is safe, comfortable, and enjoyable. This means being physically prepared to spend time exposed to potentially harsh conditions. As learned in school at an early age, three basic requirements must be met to stay alive: food, shelter, and clothing. When building a snow shelter, the other two necessities of life— clothing and food—must not be neglected.

CLOTHING

Clothing is an insulating barrier between the body and the environment that prevents heat loss. With too little insulation the body becomes chilled; with too much insulation the body overheats and, in an attempt to cool down, perspires. The trick is to select the appropriate type and amount of insulation for the current weather conditions and degree of physical exertion.

Several loose-fitting layers of insulating clothing are better than one thick layer, as air trapped in the spaces between the layers keeps you warmer. Adjust the amount of insulation needed for comfort by adding or removing a layer at a time. As the level of physical exertion increases, less insulating layers are needed to maintain comfort. The body generates more heat during physical activity. At rest, the body begins to quickly cool off, and layers of clothing should be added to avoid becoming chilled. Ideally, sufficient insulating layers should be worn to stay comfortable but not to cause excessive perspiration.

Avoid cotton clothing like jeans and sweatshirts. They readily absorb and hold water—both perspiration and melted snow—like a sponge. Once wet, they lose insulating value, conducting heat away from the body and causing the onset of a chill—or worse, hypothermia (see page 27). Choose clothing that moves water away from the skin and acts as an insulator even when wet. Wool and synthetic garments are the best choice. Have some spare dry clothing available in case one or more insulating layers become wet.

In addition to keeping the body core warm, it is important to protect the extremities: head, feet, and hands. Wear a wool or synthetic hat that can be pulled down to cover your ears if the temperatures plunge. It is reported that about one-third of your body heat is lost from your head! A simple ski hat will prevent substantial heat loss. Keep hands warm with synthetic mittens or gloves. Mittens are more efficient at keeping hands warm. Despite some loss of manual dexterity, hands tend to stay warmer if all the fingers are together. Glove or mitten "shells" of a waterproof, breathable material help keep gloves or mittens and hands dry when handling snow. Leather gloves and mittens should be avoided because they tend to absorb water from melting snow.

A white snow surface is highly light reflective, intensifying the damaging effect of sunlight to the skin and eyes. Consider using a high SPF sunscreen on any exposed skin and wear a pair of UV-blocking sunglasses or goggles when outdoors in bright sunlight.

Layering loose-fitting synthetic or wool clothes is the best protection against the cold.

21

When building certain types of snow shelters it may be necessary to kneel, sit, or lie on the snow-covered ground for an extended period of time. This can be a wet and cold experience unless properly dressed. Even with several layers of insulating clothing, there is enough heat loss from a warm body in contact with the snow surface to melt snow and saturate clothing. A rain suit or similar waterproof, breathable outer layer can help prevent underlying insulating clothing from becoming wet. Prior to putting on a waterproof shell garment, consider removing a layer or two of insulating clothing. This will help prevent overheating and perspiration, and save a dry layer of clothing for when the task is complete. When excavating inside a snow shelter, keep the rain suit securely closed around the wrists and neck, and consider wearing the parka hood. Excavating overhead inside a snow cave or quinzee can cause frequent showers of falling snow and ice crystals. Getting this snow into open collars and having it collect against the skin can be, at best, a bracing experience and, at worst, can soak insulating clothing and lead to rapid chilling. A closed-cell foam sleeping pad placed on the ground can add a degree of comfort and insulation for the person excavating the interior of a shelter.

NUTRITION

Properly and adequately fueling your body is extremely important when

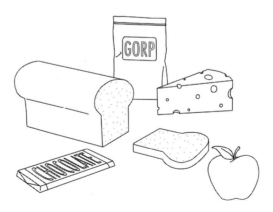

outdoors and building a snow structure. In cold weather, a large amount of calories are burned just to keep a sedentary body warm. Even more are consumed during the physical exertion of shoveling snow or cutting and carrying snow blocks. Those expended calories must be replaced to maintain strength and stamina, and to avoid hypothermia. Taking frequent brief breaks to snack on small amounts of food seems to be the most efficient way to fuel the body. High-energy foods with a good mix of sugar, fat, carbohydrates, and protein work best to stoke the "internal furnace." Good choices include peanut butter and jelly sandwiches, GORP (good old raisins and peanuts), sports bars, or even an occasional candy bar.

HYDRATION

Hydration is the process of providing the human body with enough fluids to keep it functioning properly. It may be considered part of proper nutrition, but it is such an important factor for people working in a cold environment that it deserves special attention. In the simplest terms, hydration means drinking enough water to replace

what is lost through perspiration and exhaled water vapor. Exhaled water vapor forms those visible clouds created when breathing. Proper hydration can help fight mental and physical fatigue, maintain muscle coordination, and decrease susceptibility to frostbite.

Some liquids and beverages are beneficial in the hydration process but others are not. Water is your best choice; sports drinks and fruit juices are also good alternatives. Carrying these fluids in an insulated bottle helps keep them from freezing. Drinking warm fluids is not a bad idea either. An uninsulated water bottle should be carried upside down in cold weather. Because ice forms on the top surface of water, keeping the bottle in a downward position allows ice to form only on the bottom of the bottle. When turned right-side up to drink, the bottle cap will not be frozen shut and a sheet of ice will not block the free flow of water out of the bottle. Just be sure that the cap is secure before turning the bottle upside down.

Alcohol should be avoided, as it can alter judgment. Alcohol also dilates blood vessels and gives the body a temporary feeling of warmth, as warm blood from deep within the body flows more easily to the surface, where it then becomes chilled. That chilled blood then recirculates back through the core of the body, lowering the core temperature. In the process the body actually experiences heat loss. Alcohol is also a diuretic, increasing the risk of dehydration.

SAFETY

Being aware of safety and taking the appropriate precautions can prevent injury and ensure an enjoyable and successful shelter building experience.

PHYSICAL FITNESS

The process of building a snow structure can be demanding on the body, both physiologically—coping with the cold—and physically—shoveling snow or cutting and carrying snow blocks.

Make sure that you are up to the task. If in doubt, talk to your physician. Keep in mind that even simple, everyday physical tasks become more strenuous and can take much longer in cold conditions.

WINDCHILL

When exposed to cold air, the human body or any other warm object will lose heat. Heat loss is more rapid on a windy day, making the temperature feel colder than what is shown on a thermometer. The U.S. National Weather Service has developed a chart to illustrate the effects of windchill (following page). On a moderately cold winter day, even a slight breeze can increase the hazards from exposure to the cold, including the risk of frostbite and hypothermia. For example, if the thermometer reads 10 degrees Fahrenheit (–12 degrees Celsius) and a 15 mph (24 kph) wind is blowing, it would have the same effect on exposed skin as –7 degrees Fahrenheit (–21 degrees Celsius) on a calm day. This is a good reason to build a snow shelter for protection from the wind.

FROSTBITE

Frostbite occurs when body tissue begins to freeze. In its earliest stage, called *frost nip*, chalky but pliable patches form on the skin, typically on exposed cheeks, the nose, and ears. In extreme cold conditions it is a good practice to occasionally stop and check the faces of all companions for signs of frost nip. First-aid treatment is as simple as skin-to-skin warming of the affected area; just gentle contact, no rubbing.

In the next stage of frostbite, *superficial frostbite*, the skin appears pale and numb, but is still soft and pliable to the touch. This condition usually first occurs in the extremities: fingers, toes, ears, and nose. The treatment is again skin-to-skin warming. Do not rub the affected area, and do not put it near a heat source, which could cause further damage. Rewarmed superficial frostbite may cause blisters, sometimes called *blebs*. Do not break these blisters; keep the affected body part warm, and seek professional medical advice as soon as possible.

In the most advanced and serious stage, *deep frostbite*, the affected area becomes frozen solid. This is a

WINDCHILL CHART

TEMPERATURE (°F)

Wind (MPH) \ Calm	40	35	30	25	20	15	10	5	0	−5	−10	−15	−20	−25	−30	−35	−40	−45
5	36	31	25	19	13	7	1	−5	−11	−16	−22	−28	−34	−40	−46	−52	−57	−63
10	34	27	21	15	9	3	−4	−10	−16	−22	−28	−35	−41	−47	−53	−59	−66	−72
15	32	25	19	13	6	0	−7	−13	−19	−26	−32	−39	−45	−51	−58	−64	−71	−77
20	30	24	17	11	4	−2	−9	−15	−22	−29	−35	−42	−48	−55	−61	−68	−74	−81
25	29	23	16	9	3	−4	−11	−17	−24	−31	−37	−44	−51	−58	−64	−71	−78	−84
30	28	22	15	8	1	−5	−12	−19	−26	−33	−39	−46	−53	−60	−67	−73	−80	−87
35	28	21	14	7	0	−7	−14	−21	−27	−34	−41	−48	−55	−62	−69	−76	−82	−89
40	27	20	13	6	−1	−8	−15	−22	−29	−36	−43	−50	−57	−64	−71	−78	−84	−91
45	26	19	12	5	−2	−9	−16	−23	−30	−37	−44	−51	−58	−65	−72	−79	−86	−93
50	26	19	12	4	−3	−10	−17	−24	−31	−38	−45	−52	−60	−67	−74	−81	−88	−95
55	25	18	11	4	−3	−11	−18	−25	−32	−39	−46	−54	−61	−68	−75	−82	−89	−97
60	25	17	10	3	−4	−11	−19	−26	−33	−40	−48	−55	−62	−69	−76	−84	−91	−98

FROSTBITE TIMES   30 minutes   10 minutes   5 minutes

National Weather Service windchill chart.

serious medical condition that requires immediate professional medical intervention.

The best insurance against frostbite is to wear enough loose-fitting, warm, dry clothing, minimize bare skin exposure to the cold, and keep well hydrated and well fed. For a comprehensive explanation of the causes and treatment of frostbite, it is recommended that you consult a good book on wilderness medicine (see References and Resources on page 141).

HYPOTHERMIA

Hypothermia is a medical condition in which the core temperature of the body starts to drop and the body has difficulty generating sufficient heat. A person may shiver during the early stages and show signs of decreased mental and motor ability—"dopiness" and clumsiness. Caught in its early stage, hypothermia can easily be reversed by getting sufferers to a warm environment, ensuring that they are wearing sufficient dry clothing, and providing them with warm, sugary beverages. As hypothermia progresses, it becomes a true medical emergency. Victims become less aware and responsive, possibly even unconscious. At this stage, they should be handled and transported very gently to prevent their chilled heart from stopping. Rapid professional medical intervention is critical.

The best insurance against hypothermia is to wear enough warm, dry clothing to minimize heat loss, maintain proper hydration, and be well-fed. For a comprehensive explanation of the causes and treatment of hypothermia, consult a good book on wilderness medicine (see References and Resources on page 141).

CONFINED SPACE CONSIDERATIONS

An ideal snow structure is built to enclose a minimum internal volume sufficient for safe shelter with some degree of comfort for its inhabitants, and a limited dimension entryway to help minimize heat loss. These practical design considerations help efficiently trap and store the body heat of the occupants within the shelter;

the smaller the space, the less energy is required to warm it. However, if the structure is too small, it is more difficult for occupants to move about and make a hasty or emergency exit if necessary.

Most people find the interior of a snow shelter to be a cozy space. However, for others, the small internal volume of a snow structure can trigger an experience of *claustrophobia*, or a mild anxiety or panic attack. For some, the sound-absorbing nature of snow can invoke disorientation or cause a feeling of isolation. Similarly, the light-filtering or light-blocking effect of a snow structure can also create a feeling of isolation. It is helpful to know if anyone participating in the project is likely to experience these feelings *prior* to spending a night camping in a snow structure. A good first-time test is to build and try camping in a snow structure near another reliable back-up shelter. If any of the symptoms occur, an alternative shelter is available. If the experience of inhabiting a closed snow structure feels too confining, consider constructing a snow block structure, as described in Chapter 7, that uses a tarp or nylon fly as its roof.

Snow is a somewhat porous material, permitting some air to permeate through the minute gaps between the snow crystals. The amount of air, however, is usually not sufficient ventilation for a closed and inhabited snow structure. Moisture from exhaled breath, perspiration, and water from melting snow—created by the increase in internal air temperature from the occupants' bodies—tend to collect on the inner wall of the shelter. As this water freezes, the ice produced can make the structure even more airtight. It is good practice to create and maintain an open vent hole near the top of your structure to ensure a reliable supply of fresh air.

It may seem romantic, comforting, or convenient to use a burning candle, a lit gas or kerosene lantern or stove, or other device with an open or protected flame. But it is not the best of ideas. In the confined space of a snow shelter, it is unsafe for occupants to be that close to an open flame or high heat. Accidental contact with the heat source may not cause clothing or sleeping bags to burst into flame, but the heat could be high enough to melt synthetic clothing onto skin, causing a serious burn. If something in the shelter were

to catch on fire and start burning, escape through a small single exit is difficult, especially for people in a panic or those who are partially or fully zipped into sleeping bags. If one were to escape the shelter under these circumstances, chances are that much insulating gear would be left behind. With no alternative shelter and little spare insulating gear, vulnerability to the cold becomes a big factor.

Spilled fuel can create other problems including noxious fumes and soaked garments, decreasing their insulating properties and placing potentially irritating or toxic fuel in direct contact with the body. Even if a lantern or stove operates properly, carbon monoxide poisoning is still a hazard. Carbon monoxide is a colorless, odorless gas generated when there is incomplete combustion of fuel. With continued exposure to carbon monoxide, the victim becomes less and less conscious and, unless removed from further exposure to the gas, will become unconscious and die. For a comprehensive explanation of the effects and treatment of carbon monoxide poisoning, again, consult a good book on wilderness medicine (see References and Resources on page 141).

WORKING WITH FRIENDS AND CHILDREN

A snow shelter can be built as a "solo" effort, but for safety, it is advisable to have at least one active partner participating in the construction project. With a partner, you are able to check each other out for signs of frost nip and hypothermia, assist each other in moving heavy snow blocks, trade off on building activities, and have a safety backup when one person excavates the inside of a snow structure.

When children participate in a snow shelter project, it is important to have continuous and attentive adult supervision throughout construction and during play inside the structure. Even seemingly appropriately dressed children are more susceptible to the effects of the cold than healthy adults. They should be monitored frequently for the onset of hypothermia and frostbite. Their intake of food and liquids should be monitored and encouraged. Use of

saws and shovels by children should be supervised. Although a well-built snow shelter may be structurally strong, children should be discouraged from climbing onto, walking over, or otherwise treating the structure with unnecessary abuse, especially when others are inside. When shelters are built where they later may become accessible to unsupervised children, dismantling the structure after use is strongly advised. Children participating in the construction of a snow shelter frequently enjoy the demolition process as much as construction. Again, make sure that no one is inside the shelter before it is taken down.

WHERE *NOT* TO BUILD

For recreational shelter builders in an urban or suburban location, plowed mounds of snow found along the roadside, in parking lots, or driveways may be very tempting "real estate" for a shelter construction project. These sites are dangerous. A snow shelter built into a plowed-up mound looks all too similar to any other plow mound of snow. A passing plow truck or other vehicle can cause the unseen structure to collapse, burying the occupants. Another hazard of building a snow structure adjacent to parking lots and driveways is the presence of carbon monoxide from vehicle exhaust fumes.

An idling car near a snow shelter can produce hazardous carbon monoxide fumes, potentially collecting in the snow shelter. Building a structure near any stationary gasoline or diesel engine is similarly unadvisable.

Similar considerations apply in the backcountry as well. It is not advisable to idle snow machines for prolonged periods near your snow structure, nor run a portable gasoline-powered electric generator nearby. In the backcountry it is common sense to not construct your snow shelter where one would not otherwise pitch a tent: below an overhanging snow cornice, in avalanche-prone terrain, below a rockfall, or beneath large, precarious dead tree limbs.

TOOLS OF THE TRADE

Using the appropriate tools makes snow shelter building easier and safer, and enhances chances for success.

COMMONLY AVAILABLE TOOLS

For the recreational or occasional snow structure builder, only simple tools are required, and they produce excellent results.

A common carpenter's saw, either crosscut or rip tooth, does a good job of cutting snow blocks, except in the case of extremely dense and compacted snow. A good idea is to obtain an inexpensive old carpenter's saw at a garage sale or flea market and use it only for snow block cutting. For that purpose, it will last years. Oil the blade to prevent rusting after usage. Don't even think about using your fine woodworking saw to cut snow blocks. An afternoon of cutting snow blocks will render the saw forever useless for fine carpentry work.

When the shelter design calls for piling a mound of snow, the same flat-bladed, "D"-handled snow shovel that is used to remove snow from the driveway or sidewalk is a good choice. The long-handled, curved-blade, "pusher" snow shovel is not a good choice because its straight handle tends to rotate in gloved or mittened hands, making it difficult to add snow to a mound.

An even better tool for shoveling and mounding snow is an agricultural grain scoop. These lightweight shovels have large plastic, or preferably aluminum, "scoop-shaped" blades with short "D" handles. They can be found at many hardware and home supply stores, and work great for shoveling and compacting mounds of snow.

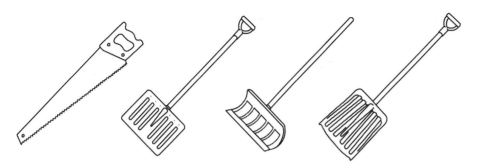

Common tools for building snow shelters. Left to right: carpenter's saw, snow shovels, and grain scoop.

Specialized tools for building snow shelters. Left to right: snow saw, mountaineering shovels with telescoping shaft, and ice axe.

PROFESSIONAL TOOLS

If lightweight and compact equipment is desired or if plans call for constructing a shelter in the backcountry, specialized tools may be worth the expense. There are a number of outdoor and mountaineering companies that manufacture tools useful for building snow structures.

Several commercial snow saws are available on the market. They are typically compact and made of lightweight aluminum or stainless steel and have very sharp and aggressive teeth, specifically designed for maximum efficiency of cutting snow blocks.

A variety of small, compact plastic and metal shovels with a folding or telescoping "D"- or "T"-shaped handle are available and are typically carried by backcountry skiers as part of their avalanche safety tool kit. These shovels resemble mini grain scoops and are excellent tools for tunneling out shelters in snowdrifts, or other confined-space snow excavation. Some novel compact shovel designs do not have handles at all, but are efficient movers and shapers of snow.

An ice axe is a multi-purpose tool used by mountaineers while traveling on snow-covered mountains and on glacier ice. The axe head has adz- (a broad chopping blade) and pick-shaped blades and the shaft has a sharp spike. While it is not an essential tool for snow shelter construction, there are occasions when it can be used to chop out, carve, or pry loose snow blocks.

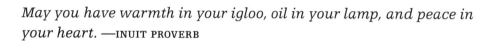

CHAPTER 2
IGLOOS

May you have warmth in your igloo, oil in your lamp, and peace in your heart. —INUIT PROVERB

HISTORICAL PERSPECTIVE

The igloo, also spelled "iglu," and sometimes called an *aputiak*, is a temporary winter shelter built by native Eskimos primarily for use in winter hunting camps. In their native language, Eskimos call themselves *Inuit*, meaning "the people." They inhabit much of the Arctic from as far west as the Aleutian Islands of Alaska to as far east as the western coastline of Greenland. The igloo structure most likely evolved through trial and error over hundreds of years, and without the aid of mathematics or structural engineering theory. Historically, they have been constructed—using a long, sharp blade knife to cut snow block—primarily by Canadian and Greenland Inuit living in Canada in the area between the Mackenzie River delta and Labrador.

STRUCTURAL PERSPECTIVE

The igloo is the highest art of snow shelter construction, requiring the precise shaping and placing of snow blocks to form a stable and strong dome-shaped structure. Two structural forces are present in an igloo: compression and tension. *Compression*

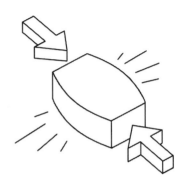

COMPRESSION

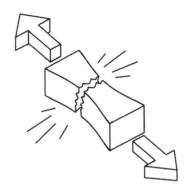

TENSION

A snow block in tension (left) and in compression (right).

occurs when weight is applied that squeezes the snow crystals closer together. *Tension* occurs when the applied force pulls the snow crystals apart. The bonded ice crystal structure of sintered snow holds up well under compression; it can bear substantial weight without crumbling. Under tension, however, the same block of snow would easily be torn apart with very little force. For this reason, a cross-section of an igloo more closely resembles a parabolic arch than a hemisphere. Structurally, parts of a hemisphere are in compression while other parts are in tension. If the tension were great enough to break the ice crystal bonds, the hemisphere-shaped igloo would easily collapse. On the other hand, the *entire* cross-section of a parabolic-shaped igloo is in compression and therefore a much stronger structure. This parabolic shape resembles an upside-down catenary, the shape that a chain or piece of string forms when loosely held horizontally at both ends.

Anecdotally, it has been reported that polar bears occasionally climb on top of an abandoned igloo to better survey the surrounding flat terrain for prey.

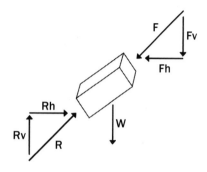

The forces acting on a snow block in the arch-shaped dome of an igloo. *W* is the force of gravity acting on the block. *F* is the force of the blocks above, where *Fh* and *Fv* are the horizontal and vertical components of the force. *R* is the "restoring" force of the blocks below, where *Rh* and *Rv* are the horizontal and vertical components of the force. For a structure to be stable, all forces must balance each other.

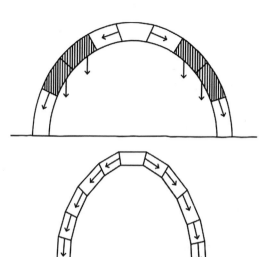

(Top) A true semi-circular arch has some blocks in compression and others in tension (shaded blocks). A dome of snow blocks in this shape is more likely to collapse. (Bottom) A parabolic, or catenary, arch has all blocks in compression, creating a stable igloo structure. The force trend arrows in the blocks represent the general direction of the force on each block.

That's quite a testament to the strength of a properly shaped igloo. Still, it isn't advisable to climb on top of an igloo to test this.

APPROPRIATE SNOW

The best building material for an igloo is a dense, cold, dry, well-sintered, wind-packed snow. It is often difficult to find these snow conditions except in the higher northern (or lower southern) latitudes—including Alaska, Canada, the northernmost tier of the United States, and northern New England, or on mountains at elevations above treeline—where deep snow is abundant and temperatures are nearly always at or below freezing. In more temperate regions, usable snow can be found at thinly vegetated or treeless higher elevations where the air tends to remain colder and frequent winds pack the snow. Elsewhere, even in flat fields, wind-packed snowdrifts may provide good building material. In some cases, recreational or backyard builders can create suitable snow with a bit of labor. Some of these techniques are discussed later in this chapter.

CONSTRUCTION TECHNIQUE

With the right snow conditions, a bit of practice, and a willing helper or two, an igloo can be constructed in a couple of hours.

SIZING THE IGLOO

An igloo large enough to shelter two to three people should have an internal diameter of at least 6 feet (2 m). By initially outlining the size of the interior space of the igloo in the snow, it will be easier to accurately place the snow blocks in a circle to form the base of the igloo. Try walking in a circular outline to compact the snow and form the igloo foundation. The inside diameter of the igloo can be marked more precisely on the snow surface using two ski poles. Plant the tip of one ski pole (vertically) firmly in the ground at the center of the igloo site. Place the strap of the second ski pole over the first and lay that pole horizontally on the ground. Rotate this pole in a circle, scribing the inner diameter of the igloo

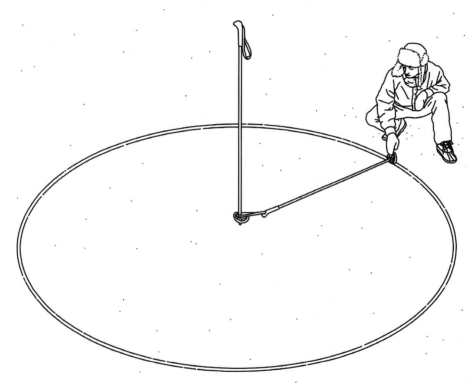

A pair of ski poles can be used to define the circular base of an igloo.

in the snow. Another approach that is especially fun for kids is to ask the tallest member of the party to lie down and make a snow angel centered on the building site. The outline gives a good idea of the size of the igloo interior.

PREPARING THE SURFACE

A solid foundation is necessary for structural stability of an igloo. If the snow surface were to give way under the weight of added snow blocks, the igloo might shift or even collapse during construction. An igloo can be built directly on snow that is strong enough to support the full weight of a person without leaving deep footprints. If the snow *does* compress underfoot, leaving deep "post holes," some surface

A snow angel gives a good idea of the minimum inside diameter of an igloo for two people.

preparation is necessary. Using snow-shoes, skis, or simply boots, walk over the building site, compressing the surface into a solid platform.

CUTTING BLOCKS

Snow blocks can be easily cut with a specialized snow saw or an ordinary carpenter's saw (see page 34). Cut all the blocks the same size. A good size for blocks is about 18 to 24 inches (45 to 60 cm) long, by 9 to 12 inches (25 to 30 cm) thick, by 12 to 18 inches (30 to 45 cm) tall. A handy beginner's aid to help keep the blocks all uniform in size is to have a measuring stick with three clear marks on it, one each for length, width, and thickness. Similarly, measuring marks can be drawn on the

Compressing the snow with snowshoes makes a solid foundation for an igloo.

side of the saw with a marker. With some experience, fairly uniform blocks can be cut by eye. If the snow is dense and has good structural strength, longer and taller blocks may be cut, but try to keep the thickness to no more than 12 inches (30 cm). The advantage of larger blocks is that fewer are needed for assembly, and fewer joints between blocks makes for a stronger structure. The disadvantage of larger blocks is that they may be difficult to carry and lift into place. Remember, for safety, do all lifting with your legs, not your back.

Cutting snow blocks from a natural snowfield. A hole can be shoveled to make removal of the first cut block easier.

FIRST COURSE OF SNOW BLOCKS

With several uniform sized snow blocks cut, it is time to place them in a shoulder-to-shoulder circle on the circular building site that was prepared earlier. Again, make sure that these blocks are placed on a solid foundation and won't shift under the weight of the additional blocks that will later be placed on top of them. To improve the strength of the igloo, each of these blocks should be *mitered*, or cut at

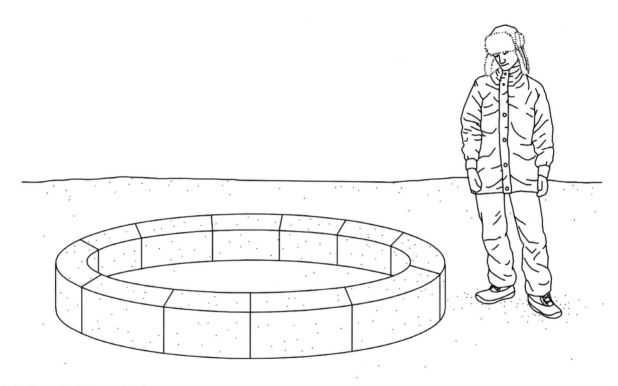

The first circle of equal height snow blocks.

matching angles, so that they fit tightly together.

After the first ring of blocks is in place it is time to cut away a portion of several of those blocks to create a circular, vertical ramp. This ramp provides two points of contact: (1) a "shoulder" and (2) a base, which will support the inward-sloping blocks that will be added to create the dome shape of the structure. To form the ramp, start at a joint between two blocks and, block by block, cut away and discard a portion of each block. The smooth and gradual slope of the ramp should continue between half and three-quarters of the way around the ring of blocks.

Shape the top of all the blocks so that they angle slightly inward towards the center of the igloo. This slant causes the block that is placed on top to lean

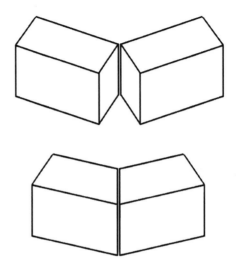

Mitering the edges of snow blocks makes a tighter fit and stronger structure. The blocks on the bottom are mitered to fit closely together.

Cut a ramp in the snow blocks. This ramp should continue at least halfway around the block circle.

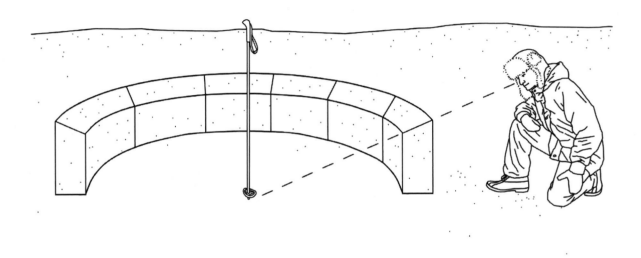

A simple "eye" check along the top edge of the blocks helps slope the top of the blocks to form a dome instead of a tube.

further inward, eventually creating the smooth arch-shaped profile of the igloo. For a beginner, it is sometimes difficult to judge the amount of inward slope to carve on top of each block. If this angle is not steep enough, the walls of the structure may not curve inward to complete the dome. A good technique to ensure that the top of the blocks are properly angled is to place a small branch, ski pole, or other marker vertically in the snow at the center of the igloo. There should be a straight line of sight when looking along the top of an angled block toward the base of the marker. Another method to visualize the correct angle is to tie a length of cord to the base of the center marker. If the angle is correct, a straight line will form when stretching it over the slope of a block.

Now it is time to continue stacking more snow blocks on top of the ramp. These rectangular blocks should all be the same size as the original blocks used to form the base ring. Starting at the point on the circular ramp where a full-height block meets the shortest block, place a block in tight contact with the shoulder and base. Cut the side edges of the new block so it fits tightly against the block next to it. Each block should bridge the vertical seam between the two blocks beneath it. This makes for a stronger structure. Cut the top of this—and subsequent blocks—to angle inwards toward the center of the igloo.

At this point, before the wall gets too high, it is a good idea to have a helper stand inside the igloo to assist with construction. He or she should

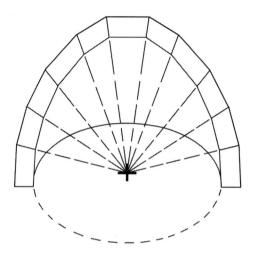

Lines drawn along the slanting top of all snow blocks should point to the center of the igloo.

49

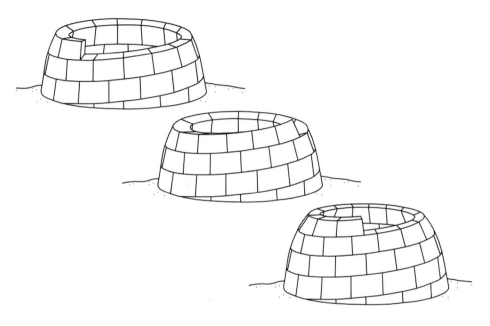

The igloo begins to grow as equally sized blocks are added along the spiral ramp.

have a saw handy to help shape the blocks, and should be prepared to remain inside until the igloo is completed. Continue stacking and shaping the blocks in an upward, inward, circular spiral until only a small opening at the very top of the igloo remains, a bit smaller than the size of blocks used in construction.

It is now time to cut and place the cap block, or "king block." This block is like a cork, plugging the hole in the top in the dome of the igloo and supporting the inward leaning walls of the dome. This block takes a bit of careful shaping. Select a block that is slightly larger than the opening in the top. Taper the sides of the block to match the taper of the hole in the dome. Carefully place it into position, being wary not to lean against the igloo walls, which could

Two people make placing the cap block easier.

cause them to collapse. Placing the cap block requires the assistance of a person inside the dome as well as some reaching and stretching by the person outside.

With construction of the snow block dome complete, it is time to create an entrance. (Making the entrance before the igloo is complete weakens the dome structure and increases the chances of the structure collapsing.) There are two choices for entryway design, depending on the depth of snow beneath the igloo: a "gopher hole" and an arch-shaped entry. When the snow depth under the igloo is at least 3 feet (1 m) a "gopher hole" entryway can be dug. About 2 to 3 feet (60 to 100 cm) away from the outside wall of the igloo, dig a hole at least 3 feet (1 m) deep. This hole should be wide enough for a person to crouch

A "gopher hole" entry for an igloo built on a deep snowpack helps trap warmer air inside.

at the bottom. At the bottom of the hole, tunnel horizontally under the wall of the igloo. It may be helpful to measure the length of the tunnel with a ski pole to ensure that the tunnel has passed completely beneath the igloo wall. When the horizontal tunnel is beneath the interior of the igloo, tunnel upward into the igloo. Since warm air rises and cold air sinks, this type of entrance prevents warm air inside an occupied igloo from escaping.

As an alternative to the "gopher hole" entrance, an arched-shaped surface entry can be cut in the side of the igloo. This method should be used when the snow is too shallow for a gopher hole entry (less than 3 feet [1 m]). The arch shape minimizes stress on the shell of the igloo caused by creating a hole in the wall.

A surface entryway should have a header block, or lintel (shaded), bridging the top of the arch opening.

This opening should be not much larger than 2 feet by 2 feet (60 by 60 cm)—just large enough for a person to easily crawl through. Choose the location of the entryway so that the arch of the opening will be centered beneath a solid snow block and not directly beneath a seam between two blocks. Structurally, this solid block header serves as a lintel found over the doorway of a house to support and distribute the weight of the structure above the opening.

Later, the igloo interior can be closed off from the elements by placing a snow block or backpack in the opening. When additional entryway protection from wind and blowing snow is desirable, a snow block windbreak or surface tunnel entrance can be built onto the opening in the igloo.

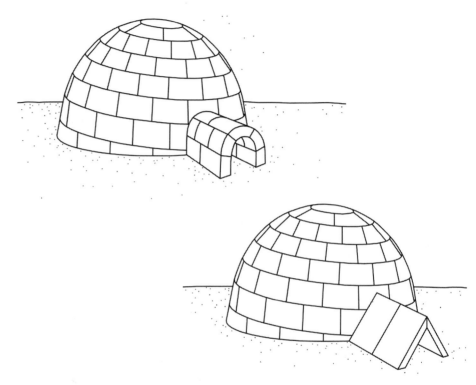

A windbreak for the surface entry can be built in several ways.

54

Even the most carefully built igloo will have some open cracks and gaps between snow blocks. These small openings do not significantly affect the strength of the igloo but will permit body heat generated inside the igloo by occupants to escape and gusts of wind to enter. Once the igloo is complete, these openings can be sealed by hand-packing them with loose snow. It is important to prevent extreme heat loss from within the igloo, but some ventilation for the comfort and safety of occupants is necessary. It is highly recommended that a fist-sized ventilation hole be cut near the top of the igloo dome. During snowfall and drifting conditions this vent hole may become blocked. Occasionally check the vent and if necessary clear it with a hand, ski pole, or other tool.

Packing snow in spaces between blocks keeps out drafts. A small vent hole provides adequate ventilation.

CUSTOMIZING
AN IGLOO

Several modifications can make an igloo
more "homey." A window or skylight
can be built into the dome of the igloo
by substituting a block of clear ice for a
snow block during construction. Placing
a small block of clear ice between two
full-size snow blocks can create a
miniature window. Polish the inside and
outside surfaces of the ice by wetting
the block with water and rubbing with a
cloth. The brightening effect inside the
igloo is surprising.

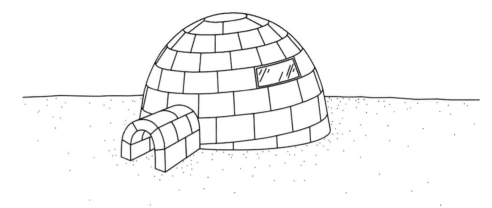

Substituting a polished block of ice for a snow block lightens the interior of the igloo.

Nearby igloos can be joined together with a snow block tunnel. For safety, each interconnected igloo should have its own direct exit to the outside. A person should not have to crawl through a tunnel from one igloo to the next in order to get outside of the structure. When joining igloos together with a snow block tunnel, use the same technique as described earlier for cutting an arched doorway.

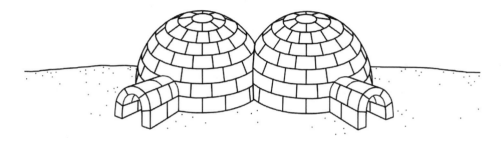

Several igloos can be connected together to make more room.

WHEN APPROPRIATE SNOW IS NOT AVAILABLE

If the backyard or recreational builder cannot find suitable snow, with some prior planning and preparation a useable snowpack for igloo construction can be created. This technique, however, is too labor intensive and impractical for backcountry use.

Shortly after a snowfall of at least 6 inches (15 cm), begin collecting the snow into a pile. Attempting to collect enough snow to build an igloo would be difficult with less snowfall. Pick an area approximately 10 feet by 10 feet (3 m by 3 m) near where the igloo is to be built to prepare a snow pile from

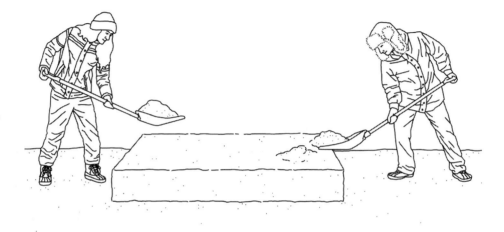

Shoveling to create a "sheet cake" of snow requires a lot of work.

Frequent packing with snowshoes while snow is shoveled on the "sheet cake" makes for stronger blocks.

which igloo blocks will be eventually cut. Shovel some snow onto that area and pack it down by walking on it with snowshoes to remove any lumps and air pockets, and to create a uniformly dense block of snow. Add more snow to the pile and compact again with snowshoes. Repeat the process until you've got a flat-topped, straight-sided "sheet cake" of compacted snow approximately 18 to 24 inches (45 to 60 cm) high. After completing the "quarry" mound, wait for at least a couple of hours for the snow to sinter before cutting snow blocks.

There is another way for the backyard builder to create building blocks for an igloo when appropriate snow is not readily available. A plastic wastepaper basket or plastic bucket can be used to mold blocks. Choose a solid,

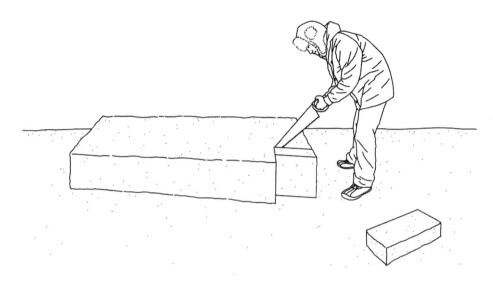

After allowing the sheet cake to sinter for anywhere from an hour to a day, solid blocks can be cut from it.

smooth-walled, rectangular wastepaper basket that tapers slightly at the top of the container. The taper will make it easier to remove the finished block. Plastic wastepaper baskets are not very durable and may only last for one or two igloo building sessions.

Another alternative is to obtain a commercial 5 gallon (19 L) bucket. These widely available buckets are very durable. They are frequently used to contain and ship everything from foods to paint. Thoroughly clean the bucket before using.

It is helpful to have several containers of the same type. That way, a snow block assembly line can be set up. Fill the container with snow and frequently pack the snow as more is added. The flat end of a two-by-four

A plastic bucket or small plastic trash can can be used to mold snow blocks.

or four-by-four can be used "potato-masher" style to pack the snow into the container. Once well packed, flip the container upside down and tap the bottom several times. Lift the container and a compacted block of snow should be released. It may take a bit of practice to perfect this technique, and depending on the type of snow used, the block may have to sinter in the container for a little while before you can remove it. Also, the blocks may need to be shaped with a saw before being used in igloo construction. This is especially true of the cylindrical-shaped blocks made with a bucket.

There are several commercial devices available on the market that are advertised to as labor-saving or novel tools for building igloos. These devices are many and varied. Discussion of these is beyond the scope of this book, but more information on them can be found by doing a search on the Web.

AN IGLOO STORY

I became an "accidental" builder of igloos many years ago. As a graduate student at Dartmouth's Thayer School of Engineering, a call went out one winter for volunteers to help during an igloo-building event at the nearby Montshire Museum of Science in Norwich, Vermont. Looking for something different to do that weekend, I offered to assist. Dr. Dudley Weider, a physician from the Dartmouth Mary Hitchcock Hospital who had spent many years practicing medicine in the Arctic, where he acquired the skill of igloo building, led the community effort to build an igloo.

Dozens of local parents and their children participated by cutting and carrying snow blocks for Dr. Weider and me to stack onto the growing dome-shaped shelter. It was a fun event and learning experience. The following year, I again volunteered to help, and learned more of the skill. The third year, Dr. Weider had other commitments on the appointed day, so I was asked to stand in for him. With the help of the assembled parents and children, we were able to construct a satisfactory semblance of an igloo. I was hooked. For the next fifteen years I have been conducting an igloo-building workshop at the museum. Each year on the day of the workshop, hundreds of adults and children brave the cold to build dozens of igloos. Every year it is a joy to see old familiar faces and meet new people who come join me to build igloos and play in the snow.

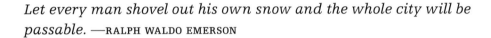

CHAPTER 3
QUINZEES

Let every man shovel out his own snow and the whole city will be passable. —RALPH WALDO EMERSON

HISTORICAL PERSPECTIVE

The quinzee is a temporary shelter attributed to the Athapaskan people of North America. For thousands of years their ancestors, and today their descendants, inhabited a large, primarily conifer-forested region that extends above and below the Arctic Circle from the interior of Alaska, through the Canadian Yukon Territory, Northwest Territories, and into British Columbia.

STRUCTURAL PERSPECTIVE

In simplest terms, a quinzee is a
hollowed out, dome-shaped mound of
well sintered snow. Architecturally,
of all possible structures a dome has
the least surface-area-to-internal-
volume ratio. A dome can be imagined
to be a three-dimensional arch (the
cross-sectional profile of a dome is an
arch). In a dome, much like an arch, the
downward force of gravity is directed
not only downward but also sideward
along the walls. Regardless of the
direction from which a force comes, it
can be represented by a combination
of two components: a horizontal
component (pushing sideward) and a
vertical component (pushing downward

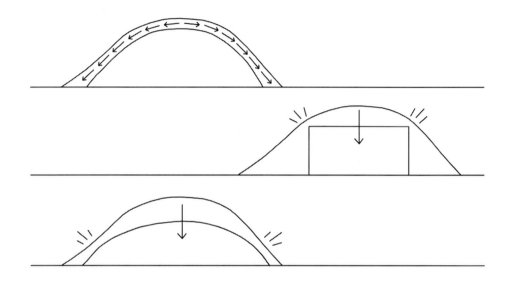

In a properly built, dome-shaped quinzee, all forces are in compression. Square corners and edges
are areas of high stress and should be avoided. A thick roof places a heavy load on thin walls and is
more likely to collapse.

or upward). For a structure to be stable and not collapse, force applied from one direction must be balanced by an equal force applied from the opposite direction. The downward force of gravity must be balanced by an equal *restorative* force. Along the entire arch or dome, the snow is in compression, that is, pushed together by a balance between the force of gravity and the equal and opposite restorative force. The restorative force can be thought of as the ground pushing back against the force of gravity.

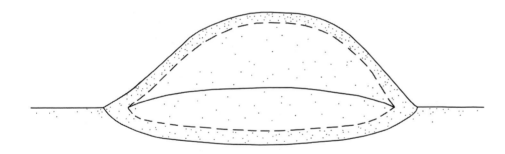

The ideal internal and external dome shape of a quinzee.

APPROPRIATE SNOW

The quinzee is a versatile shelter because it can be built with almost any kind of snow, as long it can be shoveled into a mound and packed. A simple test to see if the snow will pack is to make a snowball in mittened or gloved hands. If a solid snowball that doesn't fall apart can be formed, chances are good that the snow will pack well for quinzee construction. If the snow on the ground is already hard packed, the quinzee may not be the best shelter option. With hard packed snow, considerable extra labor may be required to break out chunks of the snow with a shovel, break it down into a powder, and repack it into a solid mound.

CONSTRUCTION TECHNIQUE

Building a quinzee is labor intensive; it requires *a lot* of shoveling. A couple of grain scoops or common snow shovels work best for this task. Before completing construction of a quinzee, about twice the amount of snow that makes up the final structure will have to be shoveled.

SNOW PREPARATION

For a two- to three-person shelter, prepare an area of approximately 7 to 8 feet (2 to 2.5 m) in diameter by packing down the snow to form a solid foundation. Snowshoes work well for this task. Begin shoveling snow onto

Site preparation and lots of shoveling make a good quinzee.

the prepared area. To save physical energy and time, shovel snow from as nearby your mound as possible. Occasionally pack the snow mound by patting it with the backside of your shovel blade. Continue shoveling and mounding the snow until there is a well-packed, dome-shaped mound that is about 5 to 6 feet (1.5 to 1.8 m) tall at the peak.

The next task is to wait patiently for the snow to sinter. (As explained in the introduction, sintering is the process by which the loose granular snow crystals of the packed mound bond to each other and create a solid structural mass capable of being hollowed out. Packing the snow breaks the snow crystals into smaller pieces and actually helps accelerate the sintering process.)

Some people find this waiting period the most difficult part of building a quinzee. If the quinzee is being built in the backyard, this is a good time to go inside, warm up, relax, and have some hot cocoa or cider. If you are in the backcountry, put on some more warm clothing, get out of the wind, light your stove, and make a pot of hot drinks. After waiting for an hour or two—sometimes a bit more or less depending on snow and weather conditions—it is time to start excavating the interior of the quinzee.

DIGGING IN

Choose a location for the entrance and begin to dig a small, arch-shaped hole at ground level into the side of the snow mound. If possible, the downwind side of the shelter is the best place to make the opening. The entrance should be just large enough for a person to crawl through to enter and exit the quinzee without difficulty. For best structural integrity, attempt to make the opening smoothly arch-shaped and not squared off or with sharp corners. You may select between two styles of floor for the quinzee: (1) a floor that is level with the outside ground—the easiest, or (2) a floor about 1 foot (30 cm) above the outside ground level—an elevated floor—which is a bit more difficult. The latter approach prevents most of the trapped body heat inside the quinzee from escaping out an open door. To create an elevated floor, simply dig upward from the doorway about 1 foot (30 cm) or so and then begin to excavate horizontally.

Both elevated and ground-level quinzee floors are commonly used. Because heat rises, an elevated floor makes for a bit warmer sleeping.

Continue digging into the mound, further opening up the interior space. A small, short-handled shovel or scoop works best for carving out the interior of the mound. Try to maintain a consistent wall thickness of no less than about 1 foot (30 cm). Another approach is to progressively taper the thickness of the wall; that is, thicker on the bottom and thinner towards the top. The thinnest portion of the wall at the top of the dome should be no less than about 6 to 9 inches (15 to 20 cm) thick. For safety's sake, it is a good idea to have an attentive partner standing nearby the entrance as you continue to excavate.

Snow carved from the interior can be passed out the entrance to the partner

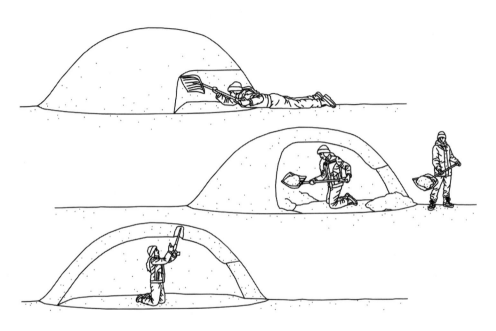

Digging into the quinzee mound can be cold and wet work.

for disposal. To keep members of the building team from getting exhausted or over-chilled, it is a good idea to trade tasks, rotating the inside excavation and outside labor occasionally.

The removed snow can be mounded nearby the entrance to form a wind-break or just shoveled away from the quinzee site. It can also be gently added on top to increase the size of the snow mound. Note that this is best done when no one is working inside the structure. Continue removing snow from the inside wall of the quinzee. As the interior space is carved out, attempt to keep the ceiling and interior walls of the dome a smooth, continuous rounded shape. Edges and corners tend to cause points of stress that weaken the structure.

71

When the excavation is complete carefully cut a 4 to 6 inch (10 to 15 cm) ventilation hole in the downwind side of the dome near the top (see page 71, bottom). This can be done with a saw or the spiked shaft of an ice axe. During heavy snowfall or drifting conditions, the vent hole may become clogged. It is good practice to occasionally check that the vent is open and clear it if necessary.

Place a tarp and insulated sleeping pads on the floor, get out of the elements, and enjoy the quiet and relatively comfortable shelter of the quinzee. Backpacks can be used to close the entrance. It is a good idea to keep a small shovel or scoop—the same one you used to dig out the quinzee is fine—inside with you. In the event of

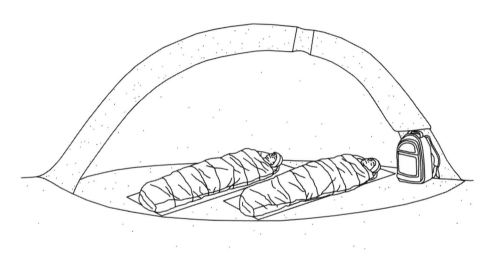

A good night's sleep out of the elements is the reward for building a quinzee. A backpack can be used to block off drafts from the doorway, but don't forget to make a vent hole.

heavy snowfall or drifting blocking the entrance, it is handy to have a tool available for digging out.

HELPFUL TIPS

One of the challenges faced by the beginner quinzee builder who excavates the interior of the snow mound is not to weaken the structure by breaking through to the outside of the mound or causing a thin spot in the wall. It is difficult while digging inside the quinzee to maintain a uniform wall thickness. To overcome this challenge, try this trick: After completing the snow mound, and before it begins to sinter, gather a few dozen foot-long (30 cm) thin, dead twigs, dried plant stalks, or

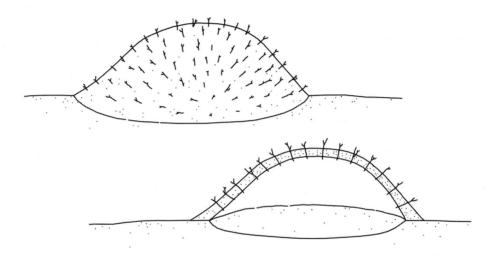

Placing twigs of approximately the same length into the snow mound will help to keep the dome of the quinzee a uniform thickness.

Mounding snow on several backpacks and then removing them once the mound has sintered saves a lot of shoveling.

stiff lengths of straw. Completely push them into the snow mound at various places all over the dome. They will act as depth gauges. During excavation of the interior, if the ends of the twigs or stalks become visible, you will know that enough snow has been removed from that section of the dome. Digging

to the point where most of the ends of the twigs become visible inside ensures a uniform 1 foot (30 cm) wall thickness.

When in the backcountry, another time- and energy-saving shortcut is to pile up your backpacks in the center of your prepared building site and shovel

the snow mound directly on top of them. Packs substitute for the significant volume of snow that you would otherwise have to shovel into a mound and then remove from the interior of the quinzee. Once the mound is completed and sintered, dig an entrance and carefully remove the packs. You will

notice that much less of the interior will need to be excavated. Make sure that the packs are tightly closed so snow doesn't find its way into your gear. Remember to remove anything from the packs that might be needed before all the gear disappears under a mound of snow for a couple of hours!

GLAZING THE INTERIOR

Some people suggest using a heat source to glaze the interior dome of the quinzee, which provides added strength and eliminates surprise "snow showers" when the walls are accidentally brushed up against. For safety, consider letting "natural" glazing occur from the body heat of the quinzee occupants.

If a heat source other than body heat is used, glazing can be accomplished by placing a lighted candle, lantern, or small, portable stove in the unoccupied quinzee, just long enough to raise the internal temperature and cause some melting to the wall and ceiling. Once the heat source is removed, the inside surface of the quinzee will quickly refreeze, creating a hard, icy crust. This is one of the few occasions when an open flame inside of a quinzee—or any snow shelter for that matter—can be considered. Be sure that a vent hole has been cut in the roof prior to glazing. If using a gas lantern or stove to glaze, be certain that any fumes or toxic gases have ventilated out of the structure before taking up residence.

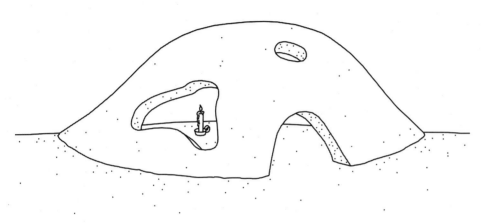

A candle can be used to glaze the inner wall of a quinzee. Always remember to make a vent hole.

A QUINZEE STORY

Before venturing into the "deep field," away from the shelter and security of the established research outpost at McMurdo Station on Ross Island in Antarctica, the National Science Foundation requires all participants to attend a two-day course on cold weather survival. All who attend humorously know this course as "Happy Camper School." Despite the name, it is a serious and intensive outdoor training program covering all aspects of winter survival, from emergency communications and rescue under whiteout conditions to food preparation and camping out in a tent or snow shelter. It is taught outdoors on a snowfield several miles from McMurdo. Here, students learn and practice survival skills.

At one point in our class, we were instructed in the art of building a quinzee. Eight or ten members of the class shoveled snow for about thirty minutes to form a large mound. Four lucky members of the shoveling crew then volunteered to transform the mound into a shelter and spend the night. The four New Zealand Air Force enlisted men excavated their shelter and settled in for a well-deserved night's sleep. Most of the rest of us spent our night in a variety of mountaineering tents. Though exhausted, it was difficult to fall and stay asleep in my tent. The nearly continuous snoring of Peter, my tentmate, the incessant rustling of the tent fabric during strong wind gusts, and the bright 24-hour-a-day Antarctic summer sun filtering through the yellow nylon tent provided too many distractions. I was almost relieved to get up and out of the tent the next morning to assist my campmates in making breakfast, hunkering down out of the wind behind a snow block wall (see page 116).

After an hour or so, we took count of our crew and found that we were four short. The four Kiwi airmen were not present and accounted for. They were oblivious to the din of the morning's activities and were still asleep in the dark, quiet comfort of their quinzee. When they finally emerged they were probably the most well-rested members of our party. That morning I became a true believer . . .

You do not know who is your friend and who is your enemy until the ice breaks. — ESKIMO PROVERB

HISTORICAL PERSPECTIVE

Discussion of this type of shelter most often appears in military handbooks intended to teach aircraft pilots and crews the elements of Arctic survival. It was most likely first introduced during WWII by military survival schools.

STRUCTURAL PERSPECTIVE

A slab shelter appears very much like a "pup tent" or conventional A-frame house. The bottom end of each leaning slab is firmly anchored to the snow surface. The top edges of the two slabs lean against each other at the top (apex). This symmetrical structure permits vertical and horizontal forces of gravity to be balanced, creating a highly stable triangular cross-section.

APPROPRIATE SNOW

Slab shelters are best constructed of cold, dense, wind-packed snow, the same kind of snow used to build igloos. In addition to Arctic or Antarctic environments, appropriate snow may also be found in open spaces such as fields and mountain locations above treeline where the nearly continuous wind action eventually packs the snow into a hard, cold slab.

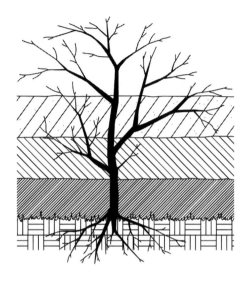

Layers of snow that form in a snowpack from various snowstorms and drifting have different crystal structures and strengths. The structure of each layer can also metamorphose depending on weather conditions.

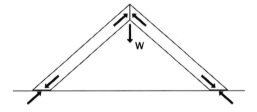

All forces on the two snow blocks of a slab shelter balance to make a stable structure.

CONSTRUCTION TECHNIQUE

The A-frame form of this shelter requires that large, relatively thin slabs of structurally strong snow be cut. A simple carpenter's saw makes this task fairly easy.

CUTTING SLABS

For a typical one- or two-person shelter, six to eight snow blocks are required, depending on their dimensions. At a minimum, slabs should be cut two at a time for structure assembly, although it may be more efficient to cut a number of slabs before moving on to the assembly stage. All pairs of slabs should be approximately the same dimension.

The dimension of the slabs will vary with snow conditions and depending on whether a one- or two-person shelter is being constructed. A rough rule-of-thumb is that the blocks should be approximately 3 feet (1 m) long and about 6 inches (15 cm) thick, and not so wide that they can't be easily lifted and carried by a builder or an assistant. Typically, a block 18 inches (45 cm) wide can be carried and put into place by an adult. It saves a lot of energy and effort if you build your shelter close to where you harvest your snow slabs.

Snow useful for building a slab shelter typically can be found as horizontal layers throughout a snowpack. During the winter season, each storm deposits another layer of snow on top of an earlier layer. Snow within a single storm-deposited layer

has the potential of bonding into a homogenous layer and potentially forming a usable slab. (Generally, the snow bonding at the boundary of adjacent layers is not as strong as the bonding within a single layer.) This condition can provide naturally-formed slabs for construction. Under some conditions, if snowstorms produce only a few inches of snow, prohibiting strong bonding between adjacent layers, it may be difficult to obtain a sufficiently thick slab of snow for construction. Slabs can simply be cut to dimension with a saw and excavated by hand or with the help of a shovel to pry up the slab. It helps if a trench has been dug at one end of the site where the slabs are being harvested; otherwise, it is like trying to pry out the first piece of cake from a pan without damaging it.

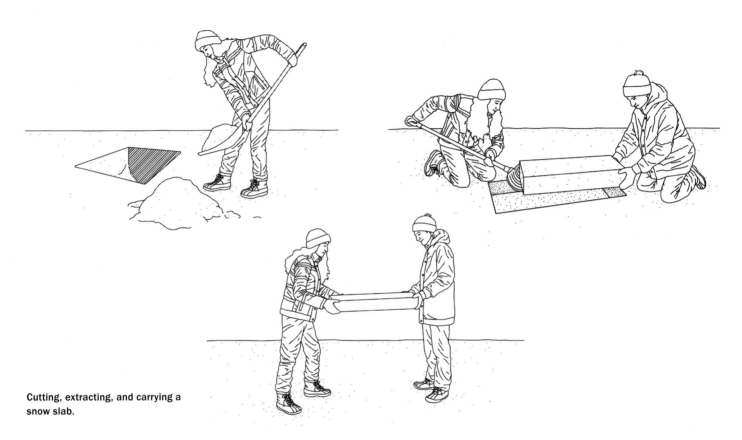

Cutting, extracting, and carrying a
snow slab.

82

ASSEMBLING THE SHELTER

If the snow depth is shallow, the structure can be assembled on top of a flat snow surface. If the snow is at least a few feet deep, the structure can be assembled as a roof over a trench, which will give the shelter inhabitants a bit more headroom. This additional roominess provides a degree of physical and psychological comfort compared to the more cramped quarters of a slab shelter built on top of a flat snow surface. A trench can be excavated after the slabs are placed overhead, but this technique is not recommended. It requires laying or crouching in a confined space and care must be taken that the sidewalls of the trench do not undercut the slabs and cause them to collapse.

ASSEMBLY BY TWO OR MORE PEOPLE

A snow slab structure can be constructed by a solo builder; however, it is far easier to assemble the structure with at least one assistant. Construction will proceed faster since larger slabs can be carried and lifted into place by two builders: one can hold one slab slanted at the appropriate angle while the other positions the second slab to complete the desired A-frame structure.

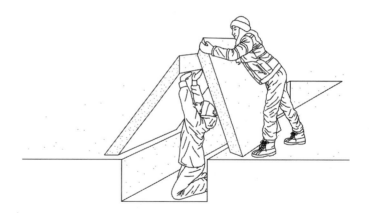

Two people assembling slabs to form a shelter over a trench.

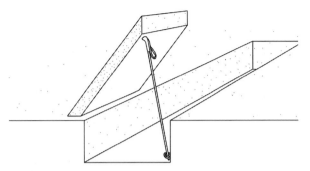

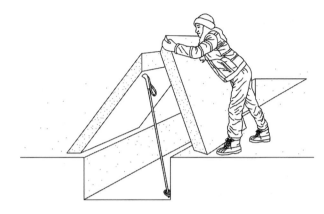

A slab held in place by a ski pole.

THE SOLO BUILDER

Solo construction is difficult but not impossible. Certain tricks can be followed that allow a single person to successfully build a slab shelter. The main trick for the solo builder is to use a temporary support to hold one of the two mating slabs in position while the second slab is being retrieved and placed. This is a bit of a balancing act.

A ski pole or stout tree branch can be used to support the first slab placed in proper position. Later, after the second mating slab is set in place, it can be removed. If a ski pole or stout branch is not available, a snow slab can be placed as a vertical column to support the first slanted slab while the second slab is put in place. Once the second slab is solidly placed in support of the first slanting

slab, the central supporting column can be carefully removed.

Continue in this fashion, leaning snow blocks against one another to form an A-frame, until you've reached a desired shelter size. Once all the blocks are in place, a structurally sound shelter has been completed. There may be some small gaps and spaces between the blocks. These gaps will

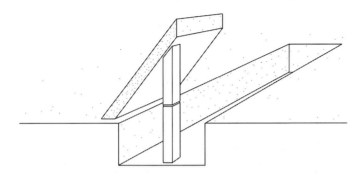

A slab temporarily held in place by a vertical snow slab column.

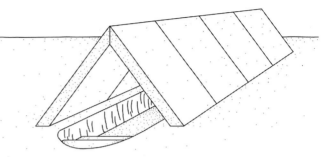

An entry to a shelter built on shallow snow.

not substantially affect the structural integrity of the shelter, but will permit drafts and *spindrift* (fine grains of wind-blown snow) to enter. To create a snug and draft-free shelter, it is a good idea to fill these gaps. Snow can be firmly packed into the crevices with little fear of damaging or collapsing the shelter.

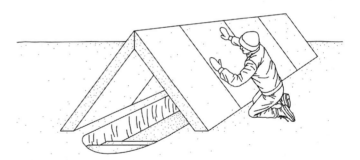

Packing any gaps between snow slabs eliminates unwanted drafts.

IMPROVEMENTS AND MODIFICATIONS

There are a number of ways to customize the slab shelter, adding to its convenience and comfort. Below are a few ideas. Use your creativity and imagination to create other special features.

SHELTER ENDS

It is much more comfortable to have a close-ended shelter rather than leaving the ends of the A-frame shelter open. The ends of the shelter can be closed off with either slabs similar in dimension to those used to build the shelter, or with smaller blocks that "brick off" the open ends. If there is an opportunity to be creative, a small dome end-cap can be built from smaller snow blocks.

SHELTER ENTRY

Much like an igloo, two methods exist for creating an entry to a slab shelter: a surface entry and a tunnel entry. The surface entry is most appropriate for hastily-built survival shelters, or shelters where the depth of the snowpack is less than several feet. If the shelter is built on deep snowpack, or if appropriate tools and time are available, a tunnel entrance can be dug. This type of entry works best for a slab shelter built over a trench. Here, the builder digs down into the snowpack several feet in front of the shelter, under the end of the shelter and into the interior. Because hot air rises, a tunnel entry creates an airlock, trapping warm air generated by body heat in the interior of the structure. Cold air, being denser, sinks and does not enter the shelter beyond the top level of the tunnel. Whether a surface or tunnel entry is used, the shelter inhabitants can block the entry of the shelter with their backpacks to lessen the effects of drafts and blowing snow.

SHELVES

If a trench is part of your shelter design, small shelves can be cut into the sidewalls for storage. If the snow is deep, larger shelves can be excavated to provide extra space and even sleeping

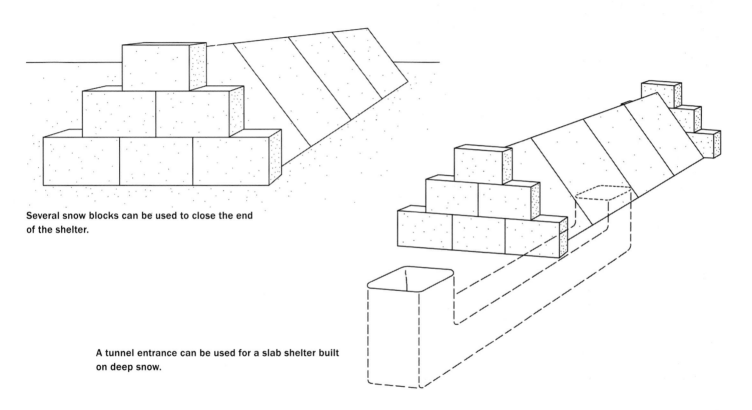

Several snow blocks can be used to close the end of the shelter.

A tunnel entrance can be used for a slab shelter built on deep snow.

nooks. Keep these shelves as far down from the surface of the trench as possible, so as not to jeopardize the support of the overhead A-frame slabs.

VENTILATION

As with all snow shelters, a ventilation port is an important feature, especially if you plan any extended stay inside. A vent can be most easily added to the slab shelter by cutting a small opening at the joint between two adjacent snow blocks. The vent should be near the top of the shelter to best avoid it getting plugged by drifting or falling snow. As a rule, the vent port should be approximately the size of an adult fist or a basket on a backcountry ski pole. Under heavy drifting or intense snowfall, a ski pole can be placed in

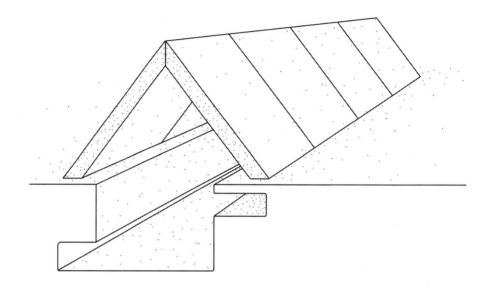

Shelves can be cut into the side of the trench, the deeper below the surface the better. The shelf on the left is at an acceptable depth. The shallow shelf on the right may lead to structural failure and should be avoided.

the vent port and used like a "bottle brush" to keep the vent open. When you clean out the vent with the ski pole, be prepared for a brief mini-snowfall inside your shelter.

COMFORT

Occupants of the slab shelter will most often be lying down or sitting up with legs outstretched. In these positions, a significant portion of the body is in contact with the snow. Body heat can be rapidly conducted away by the underlying snow, chilling the occupant and potentially leading to hypothermia. Therefore, it's a good idea to place one or more closed-cell foam sleeping pads between the snow and the occupant as an insulating layer. In a survival situation, other insulating materials

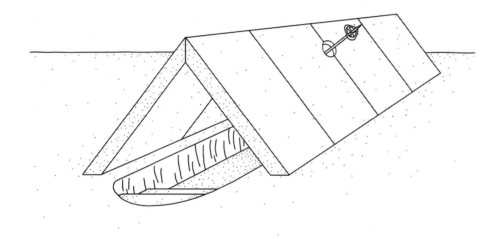

Leaving a ski pole placed in a vent hole helps to clear a plugged vent.

may be used, such as a thick layer of pine boughs or dry leaves. Respect and preserve wilderness and nature. Don't destroy living trees by cutting branches, and use this form of insulation only in an absolute emergency.

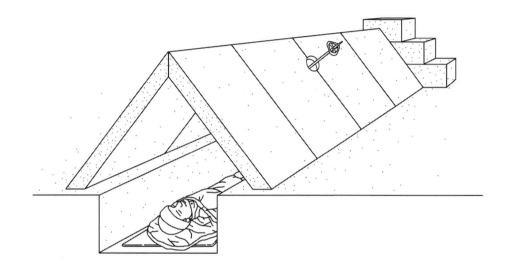

A completed slab shelter, an insulating pad, and a sleeping bag make for a comfortable night for one or two people.

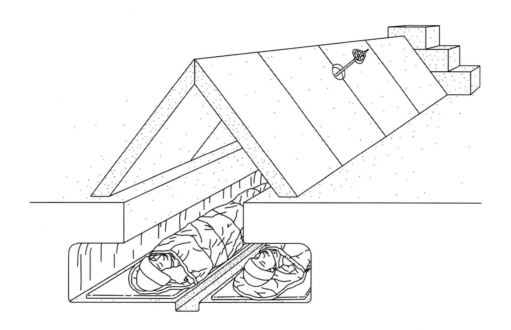

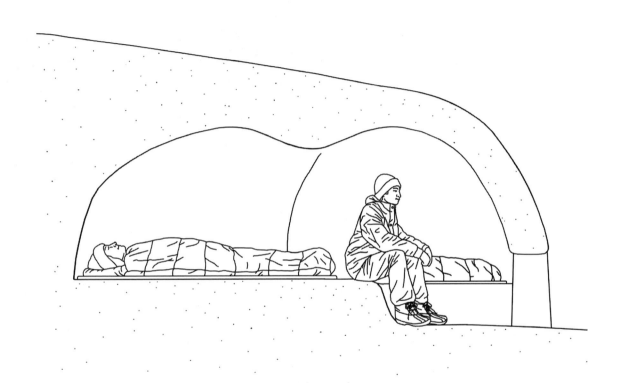

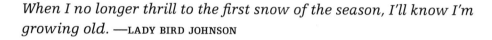

CHAPTER 5

DRIFT CAVES

When I no longer thrill to the first snow of the season, I'll know I'm growing old. —LADY BIRD JOHNSON

HISTORICAL PERSPECTIVE

Though not known for certain, the origins of the drift—or snow—cave probably go back to prehistoric times when humans found shelter in natural rock caves, or observed animals burrowing into the earth or snow for shelter and protection. Perhaps early Arctic people learned the technique from female polar bears who dig caves in snowdrifts where they spend much of the time from about November through April giving birth and taking care of their newborn cubs. Or, maybe early humans occasionally sought shelter in abandoned polar bear snow caves.

STRUCTURAL PERSPECTIVE

A sizeable snowdrift is usually a ready-made site for constructing a drift cave. The wind-blown, well-sintered snow provides solid material for excavating a snow cave. Structurally, the drift cave does not differ much from a quinzee, except that it requires only half the work. The wind has already accumulated and packed the necessary snow; all that is left to be done is to excavate a cave. The size of the drift dictates the size of the cave that can be dug. Don't get too carried away; body heat from a few occupants can only warm so much volume.

The internal ceiling of the drift cave should be a smooth, dome-like shape. Any sharp angles or corners tend to be stress points and can lead to structural weakness.

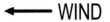

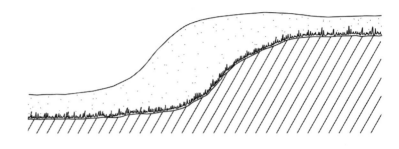

Snowdrifts typically develop on the downwind side of a slope.

APPROPRIATE SNOW

To build a snow cave, find a large, wind-compacted snowdrift. The creation of snowdrifts is terrain dependent, as they commonly occur on the downwind slope of hillsides or downwind of dense

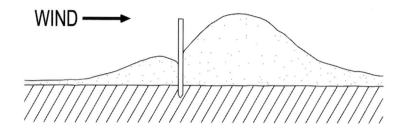

WIND ⟶

A snow fence or other obstruction can create a drift. The drift on the windward side of the fence is significantly smaller than the leeward drift. The maximum height of the downwind drift can be slightly taller than the snow fence. The tails of both the leeward and windward drifts can extend for many yards.

patches of brush. Look for a drift that is at least 6 feet (2 m) tall.

With a little bit of early season planning, luck, and patience, a recreational drift cave builder may be able to create one in his or her own backyard. The conditions needed for a snowdrift to develop can be simulated even on a flat open field, provided there is plenty of wind-blown snowfall and the wind has a consistent prevailing direction. Place a 15- to 20-foot long (5 to 7 m) section of 4- to 6-foot high (1.5 to 2 m) commercially available snow fence in an open field, perpendicular to the direction of the prevailing wind. If the conditions cooperate and you are fortunate, a drift of at least 4 to 6 feet (1.5 to 2 m) tall may grow downwind of the fence. A much smaller and shorter drift will accumulate on the upwind side of the fence. Both the upwind and downwind drifts have long "tails" extending some distance from the snow fence. Make sure that you have plenty of space for this experiment. Be careful with the placement of the snow fence in the field so that the drift does not cover over nearby roadways, walkways, or block access to buildings or other property. For a 6-foot (2 m) tall snow fence, the downwind tail of the drift may extend over 200 feet (60 m) and the upwind tail may extend as far as 90 feet (27 m).

DIGGING IN

When an appropriately sized snowdrift is located, it is time to begin excavating the cave. A small mountaineering shovel works well for this task. Begin by digging a horizontal tunnel into the snowdrift. The diameter of the tunnel should be great enough to permit a person dressed in full winter clothing to easily crawl on hands and knees into the interior of the cave.

The tunnel can be at the level of the snow surface or elevated by 1 to 2 feet (30 to 60 cm) to form a shelf. Both methods have advantages and disadvantages. It is easier to excavate a shelter with the tunnel and interior floor at the same level, and it is a good option when the snowdrift is shallow.

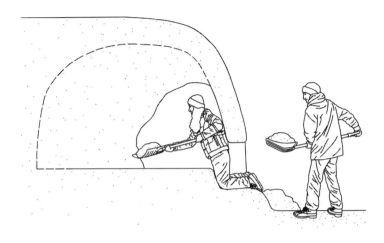

Digging a dome-shaped cavity in a snowdrift can be cold and sometimes wet work, but with the reward of warmth and shelter.

However, a snow cave chamber that is elevated above the height of the entry tunnel more efficiently traps body heat.

Continue digging a horizontal tunnel at least 2 to 3 feet (60 to 100 cm) into the drift before beginning to dig upward and carve out the interior volume of the shelter. For structural integrity, attempt to leave about 1 foot (30 cm) of wall thickness. Digging is

much more efficient with two people cooperatively shoveling. The person excavating the interior of the snowdrift needs only to deposit excavated snow into the entryway tunnel behind them.

The outside partner can then remove this snow from the tunnel. After a sufficiently large volume is carved out of the drift, the person inside can more comfortably kneel or sit while

continuing to excavate. As the excavated volume of the cave approaches what is needed for comfortable shelter, the internal roof of the shelter should be carved to form a dome that more uniformly distributes the forces of the overlying drift.

As with all snow shelters, for safety and comfort a small vent hole should be tunneled high on the ceiling of the cave. If the cave walls are very thick, an ice axe or ski pole may be needed to perform the excavation.

MOVING IN

After the cave is excavated, it is time to move in. Closed-cell foam sleeping pads placed underneath a sleeping bag or for sitting upon provide insulation from the cold snow. Slowly, the internal temperature of the cave will rise to a more comfortable level, thanks to body heat.

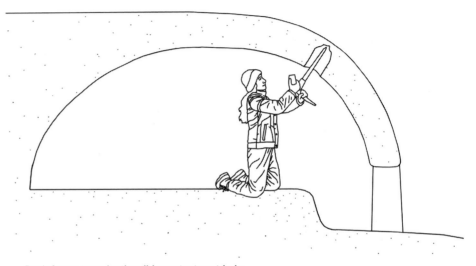

Don't forget to make the all-important vent hole.

The interior lighting in the cave will be subdued at best. The walls of a drift cave are usually fairly thick, preventing much light from filtering through the overhead snowpack. Most of the natural ambient light will enter through the open doorway. After dark, with the entrance blocked by a backpack or two, the interior of the snow cave can provide a true—but not entirely unpleasant—experience of sensory deprivation. The darkness will be nearly total, pierced only by a headlamp or flashlight beam. The acoustic damping property of snow will subdue voices and other sounds inside the cave, leaving no echoes. This can be an unnerving experience for some; for others it is a welcome, relaxing relief after a day of strenuous backcountry travel.

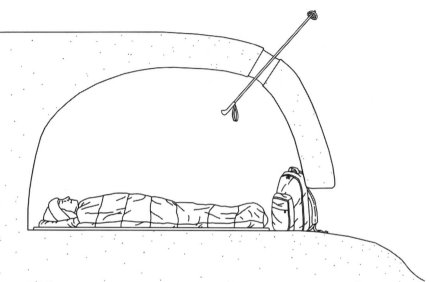

A drift cave can be built with a floor at the same level as the entry.

CUSTOMIZING
A DRIFT CAVE

A drift cave can be made more comfortable, more homey, especially if an extended stay is planned. Creativity, ingenuity, and desired needs provide opportunities for nearly endless custom features. Elevated platforms can be carved to provide extra protection from outside wind, and even "galleries," or individual sleeping areas, can be cut in the wall, one for each occupant. Shelves can be cut into the walls for storage of small items. The floor can be carved out deeper in some places creating sitting room. Basic "furniture" can even be created: a squared-off snow mound may be used as a table or a seat.

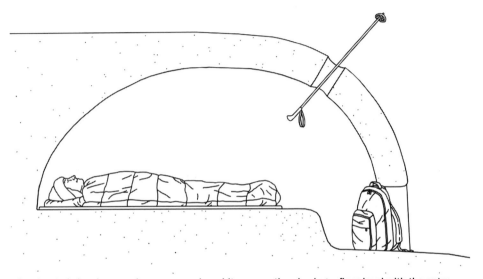

An elevated sleeping area in a cave can be a bit warmer than having a floor level with the entry.

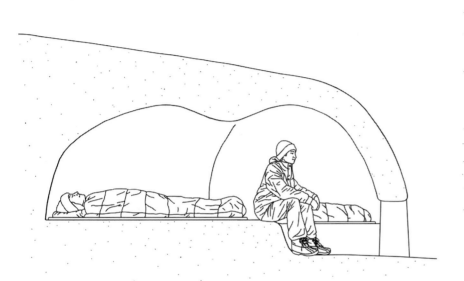

For longer-term camps where large drifts can be found, a drift cave can be quite complex, with a common area and several sleeping "galleries."

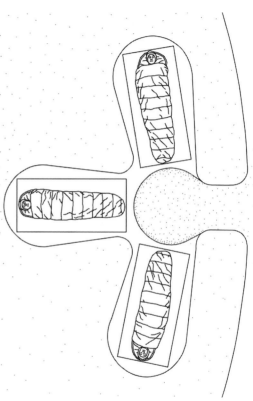

CHAPTER 6
SPRUCE TRAPS

There is nothing in the world more beautiful than the forest clothed to its very hollows in snow. It is the still ecstasy of nature, wherein every spray, every blade of grass, every spire of reed, every intricacy of twig, is clad with radiance. —WILLIAM SHARP

HISTORICAL PERSPECTIVE

The origin of the spruce trap shelter is unknown. Perhaps it was discovered by some hapless prehistoric person trudging through deep snow in a forest on primitive snowshoes or skis, and wandered a bit too close to a partially snow-covered evergreen tree. In an instant he may have found himself chest-deep in a hidden, snow-free void around the base of that evergreen. Even today, the occasional backcountry traveler falls victim to a spruce trap, usually only suffering minor injury to their dignity from the laughter of their companions. The fall is typically followed by a less-than-graceful attempt to untangle skis or snowshoes, climb out of the pit, and regain footing on top of the snow surface. As dreaded by winter backcountry travelers as spruce traps may be, they can offer a nearly ready-made source of shelter.

STRUCTURAL PERSPECTIVE

The branches and needle-covered boughs of spruce, pine, and other evergreen trees tend to act as an "umbrella," preventing falling snow from accumulating immediately beneath the branches and around the tree trunk. The ideal condition for the formation of natural spruce traps occurs when the first 4 to 6 feet (1.5 to 2 m)—perhaps somewhat more in regions of deep snow accumulation—of an evergreen's trunk is free of extending branches. This will create an umbrella-like space large enough for people to use as a shelter. Ideally, these needled branches should create a full, solid canopy, with the end of the branches sloping towards the ground. The denser the branch and needled bough structure, the less snow will filter through and accumulate beneath. Also, more snow is likely to accumulate on top of the branches. Regardless of the density of the tree branch umbrella, some low density, "fluffy" snow may accumulate beneath this canopy, but not nearly as deep or dense as the snowpack surrounding the tree. Eventually, the overlying snow load bends the ends of the branches downward, trapping and burying the tips of the branches in the deepening snowcover and forming the basis for a spruce trap shelter. Continued snow accumulation completes this natural shelter.

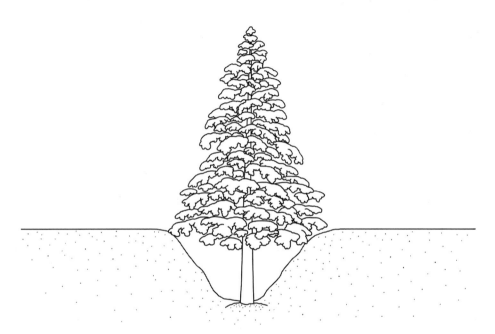

A naturally occurring spruce trap.

APPROPRIATE SNOW

Under most conditions, snow falling on evergreen tree branches and boughs will tend to form the beginnings of a spruce trap. A wet, sticky snow adheres to the branches and needles more rapidly and completely. Snow is more likely to build up on the branches under still or low wind conditions. The greater the depth of snow accumulation, the better chance for formation of natural spruce traps. Snow that can easily be shoveled and packs well is best for improving the natural snow trap into a comfortable shelter.

CONSTRUCTION TECHNIQUE

Sometimes, naturally occurring spruce traps are in nearly move-in (or fall-in) condition and require little or no labor to perfect. More often, a bit of labor with a shovel is necessary to create a usable and comfortable shelter.

IMPROVING A NATURALLY OCCURRING SHELTER

An entrance to the spruce trap must be created. Where snowfall is not very deep and where a person needs only take one step down into the shelter, a simple crawl-in entryway can be dug in any convenient gap between the

Improving a spruce trap shelter by adding snow to the tree boughs.

106

The fragrance of spruce can make for a pleasant night spent in this shelter.

snow-laden evergreen boughs. Under heavy snow conditions, the spruce trap may be chest deep or deeper. Here, a convenient entryway takes a bit more labor. Depending on the density of the snow, a few compacted snow steps or a ramp-like chute may have to be shaped. If there are gaps in the insulating snow cover on the evergreen canopy, they can be filled by shoveling some more snow on top of the branches, limiting heat loss and making the shelter more comfortable. Once inside the shelter, any accumulation of snow under the canopy of the tree may need to be compacted into a more solid floor, or shoveled out of the shelter altogether.

A spruce trap shelter can be very comfortable, sometimes even filled with the scent of evergreen. The big difference between this and other snow shelters is the center support provided by the tree trunk. This "obstacle" may make social interaction between residents a bit challenging, but is a small inconvenience to tolerate for protection from the elements.

RESPONSIBLE USE OF NATURAL RESOURCES

Respect nature when building a spruce trap shelter. Avoid injuring the tree or breaking or removing branches. Except in the case of a true emergency, the old practice of creating a comfortable and fragrant insulating bed of freshly cut evergreen boughs, while tempting, should be avoided.

A SPRUCE TRAP STORY

In the Sierras, I had an experience with a snow shelter formed by the same snow and wind dynamics that forms a spruce trap. It was not as idyllic or fragrant as a true spruce trap shelter, but nevertheless, the story illustrates the utility of this type of shelter.

Our backpacking group had skied through a heavy snowstorm into Agnew Meadows, near Mammoth Lakes, California. During the summer this is a popular campground with picnic tables, car and RV campsites, and flush toilet outhouse structures. Desolate in winter, it is occasionally visited by backcountry skiers. Most of the campsite was hidden beneath a blanket of 3 to 6 feet (1 to 2 m) of snow. We had already been ski camping for several overcast days and did not have much of a chance to air and dry out our sleeping bags. Damp and compressed goose down does not offer the same insulation provided by a fluffy, dry down sleeping bag. By the time we skied into Agnew Meadows, the snow was falling heavily. Visibility was very poor, making route finding difficult. We decided to set up camp and wait out the storm. At about the level of the surface of the snow we discovered the flat roof of one of the campground's outhouse buildings. Similar to a spruce trap, a pit, nearly clear of snow, had formed in the area immediately around the building under the overhanging roof. The building was locked but the nearly 6-foot (2 m) deep snowdrift cavity around the building under the roof provided enough space to shelter our group from the wind and falling snow. It was a long, cold night, but the shelter provided by the outhouse was certainly welcome. Even so, I think I would have preferred the shelter of a real spruce trap.

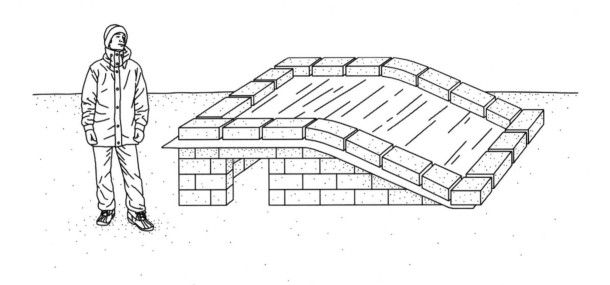

CHAPTER 7
EXPEDIENT SHELTERS

Nature has no mercy at all. Nature says, 'I'm going to snow. If you have on a bikini and no snowshoes, that's tough. I am going to snow anyway. —MAYA ANGELOU

HISTORICAL PERSPECTIVE

Not much historical perspective is available when it comes to expedient shelters. Expedient shelters grow out of need for protection from the elements in specific situations. Remember: "Necessity is the mother of invention." Survival instinct and creativity often inspire the creation of a useful shelter.

STRUCTURAL PERSPECTIVE

These structures can usually be quickly built and frequently do not rely on snow to provide complete enclosed protective shelter from the elements. Expedient shelters are based on mounding snow, cutting and stacking snow blocks, or digging trenches. Frequently these types of shelters are used to enhance or protect the shelter provided by a tarp or tent. Most can easily be built by one person.

APPROPRIATE SNOW

Before building an expedient shelter, observe the amount and nature of the available snow. Decide what kind of shelter best fits the terrain and situation, and can be built most quickly using the least effort and energy with that type of snow. Consider what tools and other resources are available to you.

SNOW TRENCH

The snow trench is a small, simple, and quick-to-construct single-person emergency shelter. It requires a tarp, a couple of ski poles, and a pair of skis or several strong branches. This design works best when there is at least 3 feet (1 m) of snow on the ground. For a single person, the trench should be about 3 to 4 feet (1 m) wide and a bit more

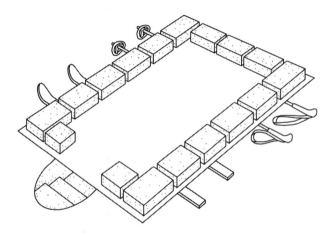

A tarp, skis, and ski poles placed over a trench make a quick and simple shelter.

than 6 feet (2 m) long. The snow from the trench can be removed either by digging with a snow shovel or cutting and removing snow blocks. When the snowcover is not deep enough, the snow removed from the trench can be stacked or mounded around the perimeter of the trench to create additional headroom. Once the trench is complete, place a couple of ski poles or strong branches across the trench and lay a tarp over top. To hold the tarp in place, shovel snow or place snow blocks around the edges of the tarp. Enter the shelter by digging a small entrance into an end of the trench. This entrance also provides ventilation. A snow trench provides a quick way of getting out of the elements, but does not work very well in a heavy snowfall or during drifting snow because the flat tarp roof does not shed

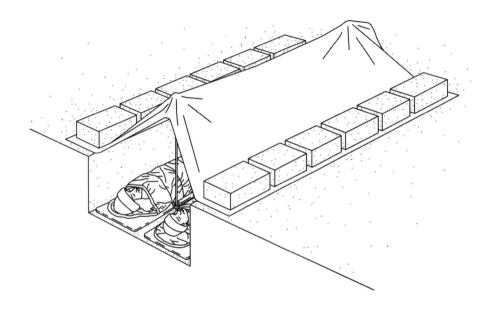

Using ski poles to prop up the tarp creates more headroom.

snow. Special care should be taken when using this shelter design since a heavy snowfall could cause the tarp to sag and eventually collapse into the trench.

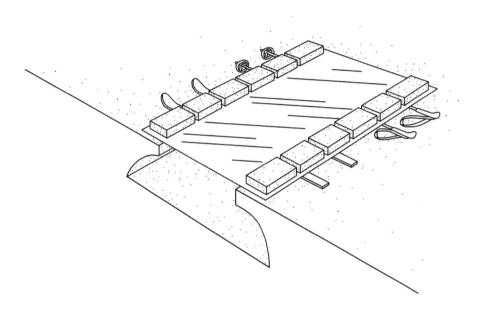

More space can be created inside a shelter by digging horizontally into the walls of the trench.

SNOW TRENCH UNDER A FLOORLESS TENT

Some tents designed for winter use do not have sewn-in or attached floors. This variety of tent can be made roomier by pitching them over a trench or pit that is just a bit smaller than the perimeter of the tent. Usually a 1- to 3-foot (30 to 100 cm) deep trench provides plenty of additional headroom in the tent. The trench can be dug before or after the tent has been pitched. Both methods have advantages. It is easier to remove the snow from the trench before the tent is pitched, but care must be taken to keep the perimeter of the trench a bit smaller than the perimeter of the tent. Digging a trench after the tent has been pitched makes snow removal more difficult, but makes "interior design" a bit easier. The entire floor area under the tent does not have to be excavated. Areas of the floor space can be left alone, providing sleeping platforms and places to dangle legs while sitting. Snow removed from the trench can be mounded on the snow flaps outside the tent to prevent wind from getting underneath and blowing it down.

A good example of this kind of tent is the "Scott" tent. The design of this

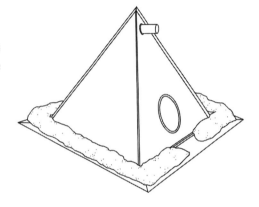

Outside view of a pyramidal mountaineering, or "Scott tent," with snow flaps secured by piles of snow.

floorless, pyramid-shaped tent was used by Captain Scott in his Antarctic expeditions in the early twentieth century, and is still in use by Arctic and Antarctic explorers today. These tents, when properly pitched, are very reliable and nearly "bomb-proof" in heavy wind and snow, but are heavy and not very compact when transported.

SNOW BLOCK WALLS

A block wall by itself can provide simple shelter from the wind or act as the beginnings of a more complete shelter if a nylon tarp or sheet of plastic is

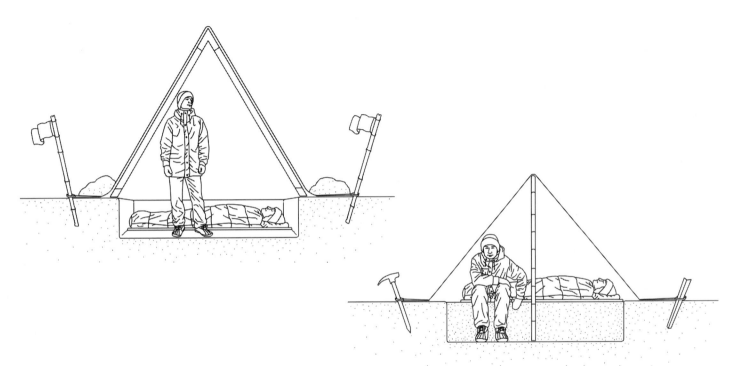

Putting a tent over a pit can add lots of headroom. Sleeping and sitting areas can be created by only partially excavating the area under a tent.

available. The size of this structure depends on the size of the party seeking shelter. In an emergency situation, the width of the shelter should be a bit more than 2 feet (60 cm) per person. It may be necessary to compact the snow at the shelter construction site to provide a firm and stable foundation for the wall. Compacting by stamping the surface with skis, snowshoes, or even boots works well. Cut snow blocks of equal size that can easily be carried and stacked. Blocks that are 1 foot by 1 foot by two feet (30 cm by 30 cm by 60 cm) are a good size to try. Build a C- or U-shaped row of blocks to create a shield from the wind. Each new layer—or *course*—of snow block should be placed so that the blocks overlap the joints of the lower course. (Think of the way

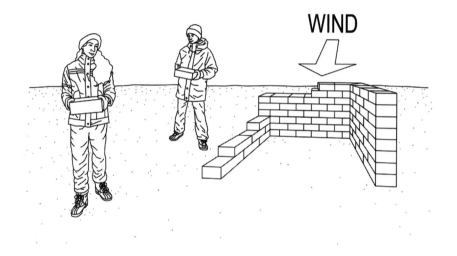

A simple wall of snow blocks can provide shelter from the wind.

bricks are stacked in a brick wall or foundation.) A wall about 3-feet (1 m) high will provide protection while sitting or lying down.

A tarp or sheet of plastic will provide additional protection. Once the snow block wall is constructed, drape one edge of the tarp over the wall. Place several snow blocks on top of the tarp to anchor it. Pull the tarp taut and place several more snow blocks on top of the tarp where it angles to the ground to complete the shelter.

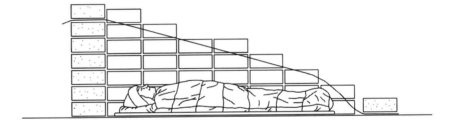

PROTECTING A TENT

Even the best designed mountaineering tent is not "bomb proof" under high wind conditions. The least harmful,

Using additional snow blocks to secure a tarp across the top of the snow block wall can provide even more shelter from the elements.

but most annoying effect of the wind is the loud flapping sound made by the nylon or canvas. More importantly, tent fabric and stitching can be weakened and torn through long-term buffeting by strong winds. Aluminum and fiberglass tent poles can be bent or snapped by a powerful gust. The wind can also get underneath a tent floor, ripping up tent stakes, turning the tent into a giant parachute, and sending it flying—sometimes even when filled with gear or people! A windbreak of some sort, located upwind of the tent, can deflect these strong winds and protect the tent. Above treeline or on open terrain it may be difficult to find a natural windbreak. Here, a snow block wall is the solution. A block wall slightly longer than the tent and

A snow block wall can be used to protect a mountaineering tent from strong and damaging winds.

about as tall should be built upwind and about 3 to 5 feet (1 to 1.5 m) from the tent. Equally-sized blocks that are cut from wind-packed snow and easily lifted and carried are best. Lay the bricks side by side in a row. A slight C-shaped curve to the row, curling slightly around the tent, rather than in a straight line, will give the wall some added strength and stability.

One disadvantage to building a block wall is that a snowdrift will tend to accumulate downwind from the wall and start to fill in around the tent. A bit of daily "housekeeping" with a shovel may be necessary to remove this snow. This is a small price to pay to ensure that the tent will remain standing even through gale force winds.

A SNOW BLOCK WALL STORY

On a scientific expedition to the Alaska Range in central Alaska, my colleagues and I set up a camp on the Gulcana Glacier, where we stayed for about ten days while making geophysical measurements and ground penetrating surveys of the glacier. We camped right out in the open on the glacier. Our two-person mountaineering tents were almost constantly buffeted by strong katabatic winds that blew down the glacier. (Katabatic winds are winds that blow downhill when cold, dense air at high elevations is driven down a slope by gravity.) Though these were high-quality winter mountaineering tents, the constant wind would have eventually weakened and torn the seams in the tent fabric. Building waist-high, C-shaped snow block walls immediately upwind of each tent protected them from destruction by the icy blasts. As an added benefit, blocking the wind eliminated the noisy flapping of the tent fabric, allowing for more a more peaceful night's sleep.

WALLING OFF A LEAN-TO

A snow block wall can also be built to improve the shelter provided by existing structures, such as a trailside lean-to. These permanent 3-sided shelters are frequently encountered along trails in the Adirondack Mountains of New York State, along the Long Trail in the Green Mountains of Vermont, and along the entire length of the Appalachian Trail, extending from Georgia to Maine. Similar structures may be found in almost any popularly traveled backcountry area. Open-sided lean-to structures provide convenient overnight or short-term shelter from the elements. Under severely cold and windy conditions the protection of an open-sided lean-to may be improved by building a partial- or full-height snow block wall to enclose the open side.

When building a snow block wall to enclose a lean-to or similar structure, do not build the wall on top of the shelter foundation or floor. The weight of the wall could cause structural damage to the shelter. Instead, build the wall directly on the ground or snowcover in front of the lean-to. Be considerate of others who may later use the shelter. Depending on local customs, it may be appropriate to remove the snow block wall before you leave. If the wall is to be removed, take the time and effort to clear the snow block rubble from in front of the shelter so that future occupants can have easy access.

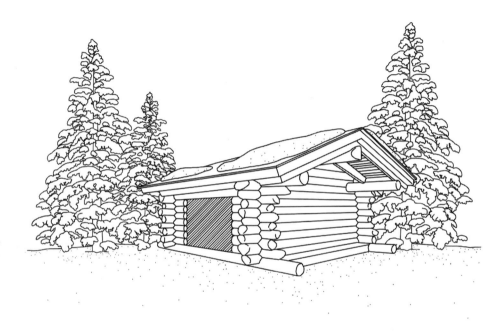

A typical open-front wilderness lean-to.

Enclosing the open front of a lean-to shelter with snow blocks creates even more shelter from the elements.

CRUST BLOCKS

When the surface of a snowpack thaws and refreezes, or becomes saturated by rain and then freezes as temperatures drop, a hard crust or icy glaze forms on the surface. Beneath this hardened surface is usually a mat of ice crystals several inches thick, loosely bonded together and to the hardened surface. Sometimes the surface of this snow may be strong enough to support the weight of a person walking across it. More frequently, the surface will initially offer a bit of resistance as it is stepped on, but then crack and sink several inches as more weight is applied.

This type of snow condition offers a unique building material for a basic shelter that can be built using few or

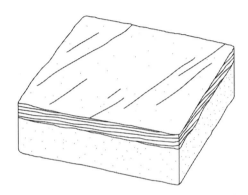

A crust block is composed of a layer of dense, hard, frozen snow and a layer of less dense snow crystals beneath.

no tools. The style of shelter built from crust blocks is similar in size and shape to that of a snow block shelter.

Prepare a stable, compact foundation at the building site by stamping down the snow crust. Make vertical cuts in the surface of the crust with a sharp edged tool to outline the size and shape of a block. Sometimes even a sharp stick or a gloved or mittened hand can be used to break the crust. The outline cut for each block should be about 1 foot by 1 foot (30 cm by 30 cm). Typically these blocks will only be about 6 inches (15 cm) thick. If the crust is thicker, larger blocks may be cut. If the crust is thinner, large sized blocks may break as they are lifted from the snow surface. A bit of trial and error may be needed to determine the best size block. Once the block outlines are cut in the crust they can be carefully lifted up and out of the snow. Removing a block from the snow is easier if a saw or shovel blade is used to separate the block from the snowpack, much like using a spatula to remove a slice of pie from a pan. Stack the blocks with the crust side up to form the shelter. Then, follow the same construction technique used to build a snow block wall (see pages 116–119).

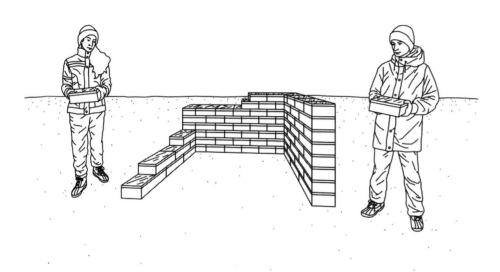

A block wall can be constructed from crust blocks. These blocks will typically be thinner than blocks cut from a uniform snowpack, so more blocks will be required to build a wall (compare with illustration on page 118).

A CRUST BLOCK WALL STORY

During the ice storm that wreaked havoc on New England in January 1998, I just happened to be attending a Stonehearth Open Learning Opportunities (SOLO) wilderness emergency medical technician (WEMT) training program at the Outward Bound facility in Bethel, Maine. There, the ice was particularly severe. Power lines downed by the ice cut off electricity to the facility. Large birch trees were so bent by the weight of the encasing ice that their tops touched the ground. Whenever the wind gusted the woods resounded with the gunfire-like crack of snapping tree trunks and branches. The ice glaze on top of the snow surface was strong enough to support my full weight without breaking. Despite the loss of electrical power, the multiday program was not cancelled. After all, it was a *wilderness* workshop. As part of the program our group prepared for a nighttime simulated search and rescue drill. Each of us was assigned specific roles: lead medical officer, medical assistant, general team member, etc. I was assigned the role of safety officer for the group. It was my responsibility to ensure the health and safety of all team members while they focused attention on the care of the injured victim. Preventing injury to members of the medical team eliminates the added burden of having to rescue a rescuer. After a physically demanding bushwhack through the dark woods, illuminated only by the light of our headlamps, the victim was located and emergency medical treatment began. Members of the team not immediately involved with patient care were standing in sub-freezing evening air, getting colder by the minute. A shelter where they could huddle together would help keep them warm. One of the team members was carrying a 10 foot by 10 foot (3 m by 3 m) plastic tarp. Without snow shovels or snow saws, we were still able to create crust blocks from the ice-glazed snow cover. Initially, blocks were cut using a sturdy stick. These blocks were stacked to form a C-shaped wall. As work progressed, I discovered that blocks could be broken free by merely stomping the surface with my boot. The construction of the wall proceeded quickly. When the wall was about 3 feet (1 m) tall, the tarp was draped over. Several more snow crust blocks secured the tarp to the top of the wall and the ground. A few team members at a time took turns huddling together in the relative warmth of the shelter, sitting on top of their packs to insulate their bottoms from the snow.

MOUNDED WALLS

When no other windbreak is available and
the nature of the snow does not support
cutting blocks and forming a block wall,
simply mounding the snow may be the
only alternative. Using a shovel or even
a pot lid, dig into the snow to create
a shallow depression and mound the
excavated snow upwind of that depression.
The combination of a depression and
mounded wall, even if only standing 2 to
3 feet (60 to 100 cm) tall, can provide some
degree of shelter from the wind.

BIVY BAG SHELTER

A bivy bag shelter is a last-resort
form of expedient shelter that relies

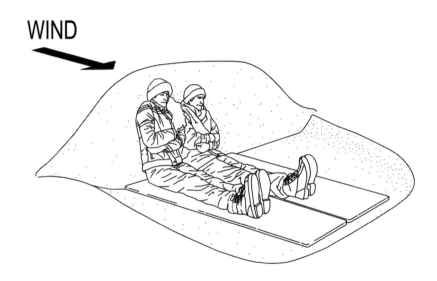

WIND

In an emergency situation with no available tools, a simple mounded wall of snow to block the wind
can be a lifesaver.

127

on the insulating properties of snow, and should only be attempted in truly emergency conditions in the backcountry. Construction of this type of shelter is taught by the Australian National Antarctic Research Expedition (ANARE). Little or no construction is involved, but it requires the person to have a sleeping bag, insulating sleeping pad, and a bivy sack. *Bivy* comes from the French word "bivouac," which means "a temporary shelter offering minimum protection." A *bivy sack* is a waterproof, breathable shell that is used to encase a sleeping bag, providing additional protection from moisture and cold.

If you observe the behavior of huskies, wolves, or other Arctic canines during a blizzard, creating this type of snow shelter is an instinctual act. Getting as much out of the wind as possible, they lie down in the snow, curl up in a head-to-tail ball, and permit falling and drifting snow to cover them. Their heavy coat of fur plus the overlaying insulating layer of snow protect them from the cold. When the storm passes, they stand, shake the snow off of their coat, and go on their way.

Similarly, humans can take advantage of the insulating properties of snow, as long as they are properly prepared. In this very serious survival situation, attempt to find a place as much out of the wind as possible. This might be behind a drift mound, the lee of a snow machine, or in a slight depression. Put on all available dry clothing and get into a sleeping bag with a bivy shell cover. Secure this warm cocoon to prevent entry of blowing snow and then permit the drifting and falling snow to cover the bivy. The snow will provide insulation. It is very important to keep a ventilation hole open and not to breathe inside the sleeping bag. Moisture exhaled as breath will lessen the insulation value of the sleeping bag. When choosing this kind of shelter, remember that once the snow covers the bivy, forming a protective insulating cocoon, this shelter will be virtually indistinguishable from surrounding terrain. For safety and to ensure that the shelter will not be run over by a skier or snow machine, it is a good idea to mark the location by planting skis and ski poles vertically in the snow nearby. Again, it is important to realize that the bivy bag shelter is only a last-ditch survival approach.

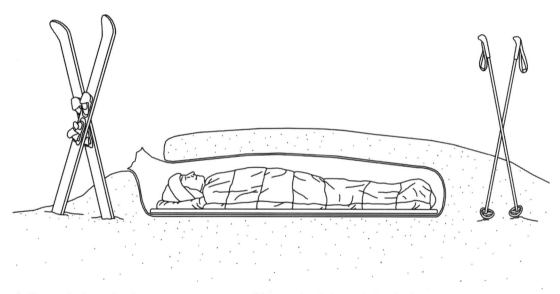

As the very last resort under severe emergency conditions, an insulating pad, sleeping bag, and bivy sack covered by drifting snow can provide lifesaving shelter. A vent for breathing must be maintained.

CHAPTER 8
CAMPING OUT

I went into the woods because I wished to live deliberately, to front only the essential facts of life, and see if I could not learn what it had to teach, and not, when I came to die, discover that I had not lived. —HENRY DAVID THOREAU

HOME SWEET HOME

So there it stands: an igloo, quinzee, slab shelter, drift cave, spruce trap, snow trench, block wall, or mound wall, all the proud result of several hours of laboriously moving and shaping snow. If it is built in the backcountry, it is probably intended to be a cozy shelter for one or more winter evenings. If it is built in the backyard, it might have been constructed as an enjoyable recreational exercise for an afternoon of playing in the snow with family or friends. In either case, the shelter is an inviting refuge from the cold and wind.

For those with winter camping experience, the transition from tent to snow shelter living is not difficult. The camping equipment and techniques are not very different. Still, even those with experience in the backcountry in winter should practice snow shelter construction and spend a few nights in a snow shelter under more controlled environmental conditions before heading out and relying on a snow structure for their only refuge from the elements.

For those without winter camping experience, it is especially important to have one or more shelter building and overnight camping "dress rehearsals" in the relative safety of a backyard. There are many excellent reference books that discuss the art and craft of winter camping, but even armed with that knowledge, experience is still the best way to learn.

MORE ON CLOTHING

The general wisdom about clothing is that you should remove any clothing dampened by the day's activity and change into something dry and comfortable overnight. Wearing long underwear or a light- to medium-weight layer of pile pants and shirt can increase the apparent warmth of a sleeping bag. A pair of wool, synthetic, or pile socks, or fiber-filled insulated booties will help prevent feet from becoming chilled. Fiber-filled insulated booties having a closed-cell foam insole and a tough nylon cloth outer sole are particularly convenient if one has to walk a few steps from the shelter to "visit nature" in the middle of the night. Even with the head protection provided by the tightly drawn hood of a mummy sleeping bag, a simple synthetic or wool ski hat can provide surprising additional warmth and comfort. This is most important to those of us who have little or no hair.

Boots can present a bit of a logistical challenge when overnighting in a snow shelter. After a day of exertion most boots will have absorbed some water from perspiration and from melted snow. Removing the boots at the end of the day and resting them on the cold surface of the snow shelter floor almost guarantees they will freeze overnight, and will probably be unwearable until thawed. It might be tempting to thaw them in the morning either with the warmth of the morning's sun or by using a heat source like a campfire or cooking stove. This thawing process can be time- and energy-consuming and could result in damaging the boots.

Instead, try one of two other preferred solutions: The first solution is to select boots that are made of materials that will not absorb water or freeze solid overnight. An example of this kind of boot is the old military "mouse" or "bunny" boot (sometimes also called "Korean" boots from their use during the Korean War). They are constructed with two layers of waterproof rubber surrounding a thick layer of insulation. The rubber

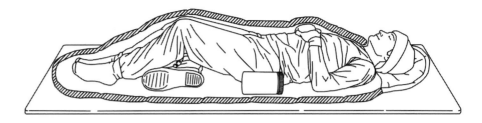

Dry socks, long underwear, and a ski cap provide extra insulation and comfort in a sleeping bag. The bag can get a bit cramped when boots and a water bottle are kept inside to keep from freezing overnight.

keeps snowmelt and perspiration from being absorbed by the insulation. I've worn this type of boot on numerous expeditions, both to the Arctic and Antarctic. Since they do not absorb moisture and are quite warm, trapped perspiration can make them a bit clammy to wear. They do not freeze solid overnight and remain flexible and easy to put on. However, they can take an uncomfortably long time to warm up when first put on in the morning.

The second solution is to keep the boots from freezing in the first place. The most common solution is to take the boots into the warmth of the sleeping bag for the night. It is best to put the boots into a waterproof stuff sack or plastic bag before placing them in the sleeping bag. Depending on the dimensions of the sleeping bag, things can become crowded.

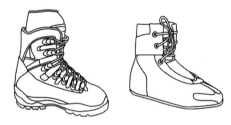

Shoe pacs (top) and plastic double mountaineering boots (bottom) have removable insulated liners, or booties. Body heat keeps the liners from freezing when stored overnight in your sleeping bag.

A slightly more acceptable variant of this solution is to wear a pair of "shoe pacs," or a pair of plastic double mountaineering boots. Shoe pacs are a classic cold weather boot with the foot portion made of rubber and the upper portion made of leather. These boots have heavy removable insulated liners that are made of either thick wool felt or synthetic insulation. On extended trips it is a good idea to take a spare pair of liners—one to wear while the other is drying. The double mountaineering boot is a cross between a lug-soled hiking boot and a modern plastic downhill ski boot. This variety of winter boot has a flexible plastic shell and a removable soft and pliable insulated bootie liner. The liner bootie can easily be stored overnight in one's sleeping bag.

SLEEPING BAGS

During the long, dark nights of winter it is not unusual to spend 10 to 12 hours a night inside a snow shelter in the warmth of a sleeping bag. To increase the safety and comfort of an extended overnight, a few basic items of gear should be considered. A sheet of heavy plastic, approximately 8 feet by 8 feet (2.5 by 2.5 m), laid down on the floor of the shelter acts as a moisture barrier. Even a minute amount of body heat escaping through the insulation on the bottom of a sleeping bag can cause the underlying snow to melt. This melt water can potentially be absorbed into clothing or other items placed directly on the snow surface. The plastic sheeting also helps prevent small items of gear from getting lost in the snow.

On top of the plastic ground cloth, a full body length, closed-cell foam sleeping pad or self-inflating backpacker's sleeping pad helps limit the conduction of body heat through the bottom of the sleeping bag into the snow floor of the shelter. A self-inflating backpacker's sleeping pad placed on top of a closed-cell foam pad makes a fairly comfortable sleeping surface. Once the ground cloth and sleeping pads have been placed in the snow shelter it is important to immediately lie down on the pad to determine if the surface feels level, bump free, and generally comfortable. At this point the snow is still soft enough to carve or mold into a comfortable and anatomically friendly shape. Snow lumps or bumps

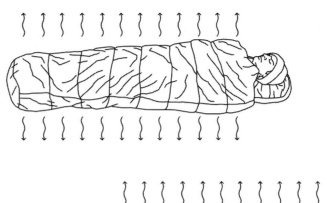

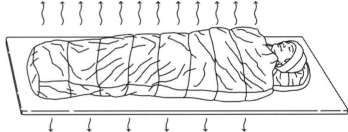

A sleeping bag lying directly on the snow surface loses heat not only through the air, but also through contact with the ground. To limit this heat loss, place your sleeping bag on top of an insulating pad.

left beneath the sleeping pad lead to an uncomfortable night's sleep. By morning, the melting action of body heat conducted through the sleeping pad and the cold of the underlying snow will transform the sleeping surface into a hard sheet of ice — a much more difficult sleeping surface to reshape for the next night.

A good mummy sleeping bag is another essential item for a comfortable night. This variety of sleeping bag not only provides insulation for the torso and legs, but also has a hood-like component that protects the shoulders and head from the cold. Many decisions must be made when selecting a sleeping bag, especially for winter use. The selection process is a personal choice that should be based on research, informed shopping, one's unique sensitivity to the cold, and by actually trying out various bags in a store to find one that fits comfortably. Some mountaineering stores have rental bags that can be borrowed for a weekend "test drive." It is crucial to select a bag that is well constructed and rated for the appropriate temperature range for where and when it will be used. Keep in mind that because tolerance to cold and metabolic rate vary by individual, your personal temperature comfort range may be somewhat different than what is advertised by the manufacturer for a particular sleeping bag. Consider a bag with a little bit of extra space inside to store temperature-sensitive gear, keeping it warm overnight. Too small a bag and you will feel cramped; too large a bag can be difficult to warm with body heat. Regardless of how warm a particular sleeping bag claims to be, if it is used without a good insulating pad beneath, the camper will most likely feel cold.

LIGHTING

Not only at night, but also possibly during the daytime, the interior of a snow shelter will have minimal lighting or be totally dark. Having a reliable and ready source of light is essential for safety, convenience, and comfort. Given the safety concerns of open flames, fuel-burning lanterns, and carbon monoxide, the best source of light is a battery-powered head-lamp, flashlight, or lantern. Personal preference dictates the choice. However, consider one of the many long battery life, miniature LED illuminated headlamps. They leave both hands free to perform necessary tasks and cast plenty of light in the direction that the wearer is looking. Their focused light is great for reading, even when others in the shelter are asleep. Most batteries become less efficient when they are cold, which translates into less brightness and shorter duration of illumination. Taking the battery-powered light into the sleeping bag with you keeps it handy and keeps the batteries warm. Always have a spare set of fresh batteries.

Another source of safe, subdued light is provided by disposable chemical light sticks. When activated by bending the cylindrical plastic casement to break an internal chemical capsule, these lights produce a soft light for

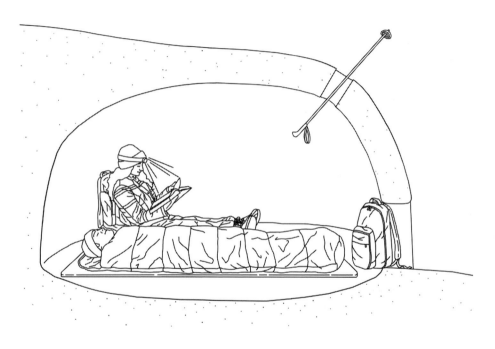

Properly prepared campers can have a comfortable and enjoyable overnight in a snow shelter.

eight hours or more. Drawbacks are that, once activated, they cannot be turned off, and the light output may not be sufficient for comfortable reading. Consider them more as a "night light" for a snow shelter.

DEHYDRATION

Dehydration is a threat in cold weather, particularly because thirst may not be as noticeable as when the weather is warm. Over the course of a night the human body may loose nearly a quart of water through perspiration and exhaled breath. Remember those vapor clouds produced when you exhale in cold weather? Moisture is contained in that breath. Replacing these lost fluids is essential. A plastic quart bottle of water is usually more than enough for an overnight. If left out on the floor of the snow shelter, it is likely to freeze, perhaps even into a solid mass of ice. Insulating the water bottle by placing it in a pair of heavy socks or in a water bottle "jacket" is helpful. Under very cold conditions this may not be sufficient. It may be necessary to take the water bottle inside the sleeping bag with you, using body heat to keep the water from freezing. A thermos of a warm or hot sugary beverage can be a treat and also give an energy boost.

A delicate but necessary issue to address when winter camping is how to deal with the call of nature in the middle of the night. Mustering the courage to briefly leave the warm cocoon of a sleeping bag and the protection of the snow shelter can be difficult. If camping out in a backyard snow shelter, a quick run to the bathroom in a hopefully nearby house can be the easiest alternative. However, in the backcountry, there are very few comfortable or satisfactory alternatives. During Antarctic expeditions, I have been issued a personal "pee" bottle for the purpose. This quart-sized bottle usually has a wide opening, a reliably liquid-tight cap, and is clearly emblazoned with a large letter "P" to clearly indicate its purpose. To avail yourself of a "pee bottle," you must briefly leave the warmth of your sleeping bag, but you can still remain in the relative comfort of the snow shelter. Many mountaineering and camping stores sell a funnel-like device that facilitates the process for women.

OTHER CAMPING ITEMS AND CONSIDERATIONS

Several miscellaneous items can make housekeeping in a snow shelter more convenient.

• Water resistant nylon sacks or plastic bags in which to store loose clothing, small items, and objects sensitive to dampness. A zip-lock plastic bag is a good way of storing books or other reading material.

• A small shovel for digging out after a heavy overnight snowstorm.

• A ski pole to keep the ventilation hole of your shelter clear.

• A small whiskbroom to brush away any snow or frost that might accumulate on top of the plastic ground cloth or insulating pad under a sleeping bag.

After taking so much care to prepare the inside of a snow shelter for a comfortable overnight, do not overlook caring for any gear left outside. Once settled inside a snow shelter for the evening, the sound absorbing quality of the snow will greatly reduce audible cues of wind and storm conditions. Changing weather conditions can cause gear scattered around the campsite to get lost. Skis or snowshoes as well as other small items left lying on the snow surface can become buried overnight, lost beneath a layer of freshly fallen or drifting snow. Stand skis, ski poles, and snowshoes vertically. Gather all packs and other gear in one easy-to-find location. Close all zippers and flaps of packs left outside overnight. Amazingly large quantities of tiny wind-blown snow and ice crystals—spindrift—can accumulate inside packs, even through the smallest of openings. Lightweight items should be tied down, anchored, or appropriately stowed, lest they become carried away by strong wind gusts.

With gear properly stowed inside and outside the snow shelter, it is time to settle down for an evening of conversation, snacking, reading, relaxation, sleeping, and dreaming. If properly prepared, the new morning will seem to come all too soon.

I grew up thinking of snow as a luxury you visit. —JOHN LANDIS

The following list represents only a small portion of the excellent reference materials and resources available on winter backpacking and shelter building.

BOOKS AND ARTICLES

WILDERNESS CRAFT AND SNOW SHELTERS

Australian National Antarctic Research Expeditions. *ANARE Antarctic Field Manual.* Kingston, Tasmania: Author, 1992.

Cox, S. M. & Fulsaas, K. (Eds.). *Mountaineering: The Freedom of the Hills.* Seattle, WA: Mountaineers Books, 2003.

Danielsen, J. A. *Winter Hiking and Camping.* Glens Falls, NY: Adirondack Mountain Club, 1972.

Department of the Air Force. *Survival,* 1969.

Handy, R. L. The Igloo and The Natural Bridge as Ultimate Structures. *Journal of the Arctic Institute of North America*, 26(4): 276–281, 1973.

MacInnes, H. *International Mountain Rescue Handbook, 3rd Edition.* London: Constable & Robinson, Ltd. 1999.

May, W. G. *Mountain Search and Rescue Techniques.* Boulder, CO: Rocky Mountain Rescue Group, Inc., 1972.

McClung, D. & Schaerer, P. *The Avalanche Book.* Seattle, WA: Mountaineers Books, 1993.

Osgood, B. & Hurley, L. *The Snowshoe Book, 3rd Edition.* New York: Penguin, 1983.

Petzoldt, P. *The Wilderness Handbook.* New York: Norton, 1974.

Prater, G. & Felkey, D. (Eds.). *Snowshoeing: From Novice to Master.* Seattle, WA: Mountaineers Books, 2002.

Raytheon Polar Services Company for the U.S. National Science Foundation. *Field Manual for the U.S. Antarctic Program, 6th Edition.* Washington, DC: Office of Polar Programs, 1992.

Rowley, G. *Snow-House Building. Polar Record*, no. 16, July 1938.

Steltzer, U. *Building an Igloo.* New York: Henry Holt, 1999.

Tejada-Flores, L. & Steck, A. *Wilderness Skiing.* San Francisco, CA: Sierra Club, 1972.

OUTDOOR SAFETY AND FIRST AID

Isaac, J. *The Outward Bound Wilderness First-Aid Handbook: Revised Edition.* Guilford: CT: The Lyons Press, 1998.

Morrissey, J. *Wilderness Medical Associates Field Guide.* Bryant Pond, ME: Wilderness Medical Associates, 1997.

Schimelpfenig, T., Lindsey, L., & J. Safford. *NOLS Wilderness First Aid.* Lander, NY: Stackpole Books, 2000.

Tilton, B. & Hubbell, F. *Medicine for the Backcountry.* Guilford, CT: Globe Pequot, 1999.

TOOLS OF THE TRADE

Back Country Access: Backcountry snow shovels (www.bcaccess.com)

Black Diamond: Snow saws and backcountry snow shovels (www.bdel.com)

Life-Link: Snow saws and backcountry snow shovels (www.life-link.com)

Mammut: Backcountry snow shovels (www.mammut.ch)

Ortovox: Snow saws and backcountry snow shovels (www.ortovox.com)

Snow Claw: Backcountry snow shovels (www.snowclaw.com)

Voile: Snow saws and backcountry snow shovels (www.voile-usa.com)

Icebox: Igloo block-making tools (www.grandshelters.com)

WORKSHOPS AND OUTDOOR ORGANIZATIONS

Montshire Museum of Science, Norwich, Vermont (www.montshire.net)

Yestermorrow Design/Build School, Warren, VT (www.yestermorrow.org)

Adirondack Mountain Club (www.adk.org)

Appalachian Mountain Club (www.outdoors.org)

Green Mountain Club (www.greenmountainclub.org)

Sierra Club (www.sierraclub.org)

OUTDOOR SCHOOLS

Hulbert Outdoor Center (www.alohafoundation.org/hulbert)

National Outdoors Leadership School (www.nols.edu)

Outward Bound (www.outwardbound.org)

SOLO (www.soloschools.com)

Wilderness Medical Associates (www.wildmed.com)

INDEX